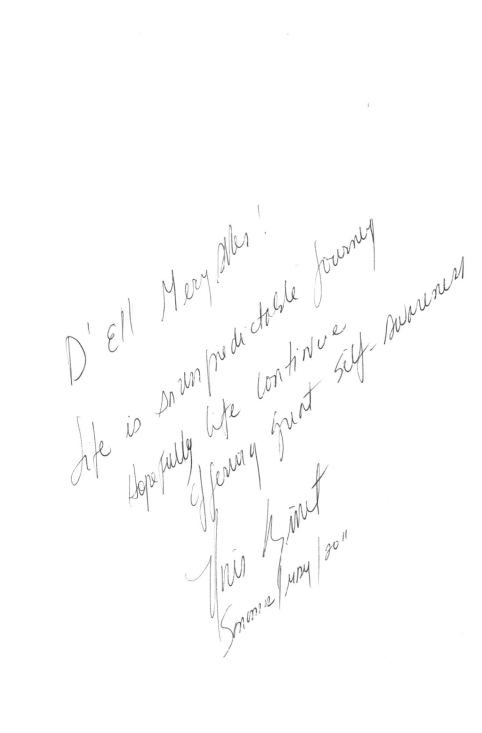

D'Ell Mery Aller!
Life is an unpredictable journey
Hopefully life continue
offering great self-awareness

Noris Binet
Summer July / 2011

Noris Binet

Women on the Inner Journey

Building a Bridge

The Goddess of Hope

Healing Racial Wounds Through Art & Spirituality

Noris Binet

James C. Winston

Publishing Company, Inc.

Trade Division of Winston-Derek Publishers Group, Inc.

First printing

Cover: "Hope" "La Diosa de la Esperanza" Original: Ink on Cardboard by Noris Binet © 1991. 40" x 60"
    Design by Kim Wohlenhaus

PUBLISHED BY JAMES C. WINSTON PUBLISHING COMPANY, INC.
Nashville, Tennessee 37205

Library of Congress Catalog Card No: 92-60850
ISBN: 1-55523-646-6

Printed in the United States of America

For my sister Carmen Emilia,
A mi hermana,

and to every one of you
my sisters.

From the Heart
—Noris Binet

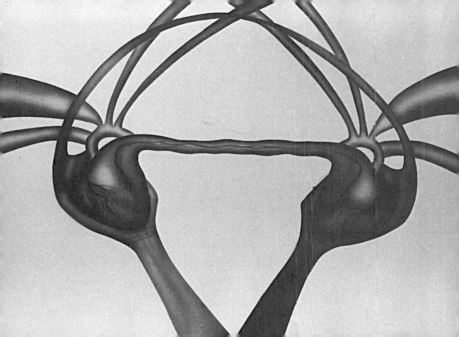

Women on the Inner Journey

Building A Bridge

"Women on the Inner Journey" is a continuous process of transformation, a journey that is never finished, never complete, never perfect. It's about being alive, about nurturing, sharing, supporting, touching, dancing, creating, laughing, reaching out, building bridges, healing wounds.

It's about becoming fully human.

"Black and White Women Building a Bridge, 500 years in the Land of the Native American" is an ongoing multimedia project of *Women on the Inner Journey* that began in May 1992 in Nashville, Tennessee. It is a process for creating a safe and sacred place where African Americans and European Americans can explore healing.

Acknowledgements

I wish to thank all those who have helped me complete this book,
in particular:

Brock Mehler, for his unconditional care and his patience in editing.

Penny Case, for her indispensable contribution: writing, editing and coordinating
the production of this book. For her companionship, patience and support which
helped to keep me going.

Angela Smith, for creating the colors and design. Without her this book could not
have been done. For her courage to commit herself without knowing me, just
because she believed in this vision.

To all the *Artists* who contributed their artwork.

Gwynelle Dismukes, for her enthusiasm, emotional support and special friendship.

Mary Elizabeth Townsell, for her gentle friendship and her spiritual awareness that
remind me over and over to be in touch with my spiritual center.

Nancy LeQuire, for her nurturing and loving friendship, supporting me always in my
incursion into this culture.

Jairo Prado, whose presence in my life and my work has been a source of inspiration
and growth.

Huemac, for sharing his knowledge and initiating me into the world of art and magic.

Renee LaRose, for her special contribution and solidarity, nurturing my creativity.

Karen Callis, for her unconditional support in my process, helping me to plant my
Latin American roots in the heart.

George Bullard, for his supporting friendship.

Carlton Wilkinson, for being the first African-American friend in this country, and
supporting me in my projects.

Maxime Beach, for nurturing the female energy in me and believing in my integrity.

LifeWorks Foundation, for the substantial support and belief in this vision.

Isabel Fuente, for her supporting and nurturing friendship.

MaryAnne Howland, for her professional contribution, which greatly improved this
book.

The realization of this project was made possible by the efforts of many women. My
deep thanks to all of you: *Johnnie Enloe, Pat Smith, Jane Fleishman, Susan Canon,
Lynda Bates, Sydney Reichman, Jane Braddock, Julie Luckett, Margaret Meggs, Joan
French, Sharon R. Cohen and Dene Berry.*

Special thanks to all of you who may not be mentioned here, but I carry you in my
heart.

And finally, I give my thanks to the different spiritual guides that are present in my
life, and to the Goddess Athena for helping me to focus my energy and complete this
book.

Visions

Can

Come

True

Building bridges has been one of the greatest engineering challenges that humans have faced in the construction of their societies. Each time they encounter separation—because of water, a canyon or any other condition, they have to stop until they are able to develop a way to fill the gap, to cross from one side to the other.

I sense that moment is very exciting for them, to be able to go beyond the cliff. The process that happens in their physical life reflects and forces a process that happens in their inner life too; that is why the "bridge" is one of the most universal extended symbols.

"The two banks of the river to be crossed by the bridge represent the two worlds of mortality and death, immortals and life; the bridge is the passage from death to immortality, from the unreal to the real."*

"Communication between heaven and earth, one realm and another, unifying the human with the divinity."†

We see that we are always dealing with a logical, physical perception and with another that is illogical, poetic and symbolic.

This project explores the multifaceted aspects of bridges. It is not only the physical bridge created by the very existence of the artwork of this group of women, but that this group of women worked together in several workshops building emotional and spiritual bridges and exploring one of the most important bridges, the one that each individual started to build with herself, with her body, with her inner self, with her creative process and her healing energy.

It is almost impossible to judge what is growing and what is in the process of becoming; therefore this was a non-juried exhibit. Every artist selected her piece, and what she chose is reproduced here.

Rainer Maria Rilke was very assertive when he said "works of art are of an infinite loneliness and no means of approach is so useless as criticism. Only love can grasp and hold and be just toward them."*

Let's be thankful to the Divine that offers us this opportunity to be together and share. I invite you to dedicate this time not only for the healing between black and white, but to recognize that both black and white are immigrants in the land of the Native Americans, who still, five hundred years later, are suffering from being homeless in their own land.

This is a Sacred Moment.

Thank you,
Noris Binet

* *Diccionario de los Símbolos*, 1986.
† An *Illustrated Encyclopaedia of Traditional Symbols*, 1978.
Letters to a Young Poet.

Contents

EPILOGUE

From the Mother of the Earth

An Offering

Everything that we do is the reflection of our soul in the mirror of the eyes of each human being.

It is like a birthing in which we all have participated.

I offer this work to you, my brother, to you, my sister, who have been my companions throughout this uncertain journey of existence; you who gave me your hands to help me cross the profound abyss.

I am part of you. Your search is my own, and your fears are my own fears. Everything that has happened to you is the same thing that has happened to me.

This reflection of my soul is also the reflection of yours; this that I created, you created with me . . . in my lonely nights, touching the profound solitude, you have been present in your own solitude, and together we have created this mirror in which today we look at ourselves.

Introduction

European colonization of the new world, which was already home to an estimated 72 million indigenous people, seven million of them living on the North American continent, began in 1492, 500 years ago. For many of you this only means an historical time, printed in a newspaper, magazine or book. For others of us, it means not only the end of an epoch and the birth of a new race, but the tragic massacre of an ancestral culture, a culture which in many aspects acknowledged that human life is a part of the universe, One with the endless and infinite stream of life.

Many of the white men who came were intent on exterminating the natives of this new world, and hunting and enslaving the African people.

In the name of this new race, born not only from violence, pain, rape and blood, but from fascination, passion and fire, I wish to speak. I want to share with you my dreams and my visions of a world we create day by day, with our actions, with our lives.

Life always plays interesting games with us. It takes us through complex labyrinths. It sometimes shakes us so deeply that we lose not only faith if we have it, but our certainty that we will survive. And many times, we don't have a clue why. "Why to me? Why did this happen to me?" we repeat. "Why to me?" we scream louder. "Why was I born in this kind of place? In this kind of culture? In this kind of world? In this social class? In this kind of body?"

As a Dominican woman living in the United States, the question "Why am I in this culture, in this country?" has been my companion for the last few years. The answer has been coming to me in very small pieces, sometimes uncertain, other times very clear and profound, like a revelation. In my pain from this cultural shock and process of adjustment, I have been forced to utilize all my resources to be able to keep a certain amount of mental sanity.

While I seldom understood how it could be happening, the pieces were slowly coming together. At the same time, I knew that hidden forces were leading me. I did not always know how to surrender to those forces, which provoked uncertainty and confusion in me. Working with women has been a constant, and through that work I became more clear about what I am to do. Now, working toward the restoration of the feminine principle on the planet is becoming a very important commitment in my life.

Woman is the seed containing the potential for the growth of new life. Her feminine nature is cyclic, corresponding to the cycles of the moon. The intuitive power within her grows toward fulfillment from the beginning of the cycle until ovulation, then wanes toward introspection from ovulation to menstruation. In this intimate process, shared by every woman, no matter what her color, she gives to herself the opportunity to be born again.

My practice in facilitating and teaching individuals and groups in therapeutic dance, movement for personal transformation, expressive arts, rituals and healing has been a very important door through which have come answers. In the daily practice of this work I have found very clearly why I am here.

This work has allowed me to witness, and understand from the inside, the pain and contradiction of this society. Through facilitating this work I have experienced the need in individuals for communication on a deeper level, for touching, for spontaneity, for community, for change, for living in a more human way, for an authentic spiritual celebration.

I have also been receiving answers as to what kind of contribution I can make to this society. The creation of this project, "Black and White Building a Bridge" has shown me that in this way my energy can be properly used. Here I can synthesize the different aspects of my work, from the individual to the collective, from creativity to healing. Here I can bring a vision of life to help others understand the beauty in something as simple as a way of walking when the pelvis has the rhythm of the steps.

In the course of investigating the viability of this project, I realized that not only the community of Nashville, but the whole country as well, was ready to go beyond an attitude of charity and condescension toward black people. What is lacking with regard to the black community is human contact on a deeper, more sincere level, the level that recognizes our common humanity and acknowledges that everything that is born dies; everything that dies transcends; and all of us now alive will also someday die.

This book is a visual and literary record of our process in creating this project. At the same time, it explains and suggests how this same process can be created in other communities.

There are not many books about women's artwork, and very little about what women are creating at this moment. It is my strong desire to create here not only a catalog of the exhibit, but also space in which the reader can become engaged in each of the different steps and be a part of it, too. Why? Because this project is about a process of transformation that is life; never finished, never complete, never perfect. It is about being alive, about nurturing, sharing, supporting, touching, dancing, creating, laughing, reaching out, building bridges, healing wounds, becoming fully human.

Perhaps the most essential part of this project is that it is created and developed by common people who believe that something can be done to create change. Using only their personal resources, they are taking responsibility for creating a better place to live. It is time for people from small places to be heard. It is not only people in cosmopolitan urban areas who have options to offer.

Small cities have courage, too. That sometimes surprises us. Nashville is one of those surprises. This southern city, with its history of racism, is the birthplace of this project. Black and White Building a Bridge is a baby yet, but with the proper care and nourishment, it will grow. This book provides a foundation for us to serve and support each of you who are wishing to find a way to bring more compassion into the world.

Noris Binet

The

Vision

Manifested

The Vision

When I moved to Nashville from Mexico in 1988, one of the first places my husband took me to visit was the Parthenon. He knew I would enjoy this reproduction of the 5th century B.C. Greek temple to the goddess Athena. The architecture of the Parthenon, like that of other sacred temples and pyramids, is an expression of the relationship between the human and the divine expressed in a single form. Being in such places always evokes the sensation of being in the presence of something beyond yourself. The Parthenon is not just a building, but a high point in human consciousness, and an important legacy from our ancestors.

I made two connections during that first visit which have powerfully influenced the direction of my work since then.

The first was with the archetypal energy of the goddess Athena. This connection came not only through my presence in her temple, but also through the growing presence of a colossal statue of Athena, which was in the last stage of a seven-year creative effort by Nashville sculptor Alan LeQuire.

The other connection came to me as a vision. I saw something at the Parthenon that I didn't see happening in any other place in Nashville. I saw black and white together, sharing the same space in a very relaxed way. I really felt good seeing that. Almost immediately I envisioned a performance in the temple with black and white artists. I thought this would be very powerful visually, because darkness and light together create the whole.

People reacted very strongly to my idea. They said,

Photograph by Carlton Wilkinson

"In Nashville? Black and white people performing in the Parthenon? Forget it!"

Although many people tried to discourage me, my vision to bring black and white together in some healing way was strong. I began working at the Parthenon with my friend, Nancy LeQuire, and Michael Gambrell. I created a series of images which were photographed by Carlton Wilkinson: "The Parthenon from Another Point of View," a project which is still in process.

At this point I began to realize that there was a profound absence of black artists in the mainstream Nashville art community. This was very disturbing to me. I come from a highly mixed culture where, despite the vestiges of racism, African, European and Native American intermarry. Here, there is separation of races. The African-American seems like a ghost if you are looking from the white world. Something is missing here. Something is dehumanized.

I can understand the nature of this conflict because from a very early age I knew I was a person of mixed race. It is painful to see what is happening here. These three races are each isolated; a person must be one color or the other. A person of mixed race is forced to choose. The reality is that some of us are a mix of four or five races. We have not only to acknowledge these different races in ourselves, but to heal them, make peace among them and eventually love them.

Interacting with close friends and discussing my point of view about the racial condition, I found that some white people wanted to be more in touch with African-Americans, but their culture offered no opportunity for this to happen. Also, the majority of white people do not realize what is happening between the races. Everybody is so accustomed, so well adjusted to the habit of seeing African-Americans as people in the background of their lives, that it was very difficult to find forums where I could bring the subject into the light.

I was often angry, because I, too, felt a good deal of discrimination because of my color. I was slow to realize this, because the U.S. is the first place where I have felt something was wrong because of my race. Still, it was clear that I could not allow my own frustration to influence my actions. It was not my wish to get trapped into reacting on the basis of such emotions.

Because of my mixed race and spiritual heritage, I understood that I couldn't view life from such a narrow perspective, that the challenge is to go beyond that and bring the energy of shared diversity, helping others to see that if all cultures take the time to know each other, surprises will happen and we will be walking on a new path. I believe such a change is the only one, right now, that is capable of answering some of our deepest questions: "Why are we here?" "How can we keep from destroying this planet and ourselves?" "How do we learn the lesson of forgiveness and love?"

Invoking spiritual energy for the purpose of transforming our physical world is a practice as old as human life. When human beings encounter a major catastrophe, or conditions which are unchangeable, they come back to the way of their ancestors and ask the divine forces for help and guidance. In many cultures this is a very important practice in daily life. I come from a tradition that shares these principles.

Since that first connection at the Parthenon, I began to investigate who this goddess Athena really was, and why she is being reborn thousands of years later in Nashville, in the new continent, in the new world. For this question I have found only clues, not a definitive answer. I discovered that Athena entered into partnerships with humans to help them in their endeavors. Because her image was so close and accessible to me (as pyramids had been in Mexico), I began working in my own psyche to activate her archetypal energy.

At the same time, I interacted with different women's groups in gatherings and rituals. I found in all of them a common need for community and for exploration around the idea of sharing and supporting. They have a strong need to discuss how it was when women were not abused, raped and killed just because they were women; how it was when women were respected, how it was when women had an important place in the spiritual guidance of their communities, when they were the ones who helped other women to bring new life into existence; when it was natural, pleasurable and socially accepted to breast-feed their babies.

Since I grew up in a culture in which some of these aspects are still alive (though in the process of becoming extinct), I felt that I could offer some of my cultural heritage as well as learn and receive some of the benefits of this culture. I wanted to create a space where women could feel comfortable being women, and in particular being women searching for their spiritual identities.

The process of becoming an artist is endless. I always have my eyes open for new creations and new ideas in germination. At the gatherings I was exposed to some of the women's creations, and their images spoke to me

from an archetypal world. I believed it was important for the community to see these images, and for the women to see the value of their own creations and the creations of other women, and so as my first step I arranged an exhibit of their work.

"Women on the Inner Journey" was the name that came to me for the exhibit, for the simple reason that all of them were in some kind of inner process. The goal of this first exhibit was to bring together a group of creative women from different backgrounds to share with the community a new vision about art, healing and spirituality.

As part of the exhibit we created an altar in the gallery, reminding us that every act can be sacred if we intend so. The altar, created by Margaret Meggs, was a great gift, a place that held the energy of the artists and the public. This country was then at war in the Middle East, and the altar also provided a place where everyone could write their wish for peace in the world.

Many times during the opening reception people said to me, "Women are thirsty for something like this."

In this first exhibit, most of the women artists were white. That was all right because it was a reflection of that part of the culture with which I was involved. It was an important step in my process of working in the art community, and it provided the foundation for creating my vision of bringing black and white together.

* * *

Symbols are a very important part of my work. We humans are a symbolical species. Through symbols we can transform ourselves and the world around us, and that has been true since the beginning of our time on this planet. One of the things the goddess Athena symbolizes is a new order in society. My vision of a new order is one in which the focus is on a deeper connection to the creative spiritual center of our being.

Participating in a Jean Houston workshop in Nashville centered around Athena, I was able to go further in the process and experience a more profound initiation into the archetypal Athena energy. For the first time I could dance and create my own ritual inside of the temple.

Since that experience, I became more involved in my relationship with Athena, exploring the multifaceted aspects of the journey. At the same time, people interested in participating in the Black and White project started coming into my life. That is when I

Noris Binet

met Angela Smith, the designer of this book.

In this process I reaffirmed that when we are able to open ourselves to the world of symbols, we can reconnect with a psychic aspect of life that has been forgotten in modern societies. In this country people are realizing more and more that we are living in a very catastrophic time. For some individuals it is so overwhelming to cope with the daily worries of economic stress, abuse and dissatisfaction with their "successful" lives that they give up trying to do something about conditions. Most of the time they don't think they have the power to really make a difference. Part

Photograph by Carlton Wilkinson

of the contribution of this project is to help people understand that we can actually transform our limitations, that there are things anybody can do. All that is needed is to believe it. It's that simple.

That simple belief is difficult for people in this society because individuals have been cut off from their inner creative power. Except for a few who are far outside the mainstream, this society has no healers. Western society is the only culture I know about that killed its women because they were healers. Because of this incredible catastrophe, the healing energy of many men and women has no place to go, as it does in other cultures. We must explore how a reconnection to inner power can be made, create a place for it to be and begin to heal this culture's deep, historical wound. The wound must be healed for change to take place. We have the responsibility to

work in the world to bring about a condition in which rituals can have meaning and our lives are sacred in all aspects, from making love, to work, to giving birth, to creating, even though the system is breaking into pieces and everything appears to be in chaos.

In my culture it is women—beginning with my own mother—who have modeled for me the creation of social change. It is women who organize the school, the spiritual life, all the activities that hold the community together. More than anything else they work for resolution and peace.

Artists—real artists—have always been pioneers, those who have no boundaries. They reach out of their original culture and find their home in foreign places, physically or internally. It is the artists who, out of the depth of the human unconscious, from a faraway point outside of society, can communicate with the whole of humanity.

I feel that women artists, now, can provide a matrix from which new possibilities can spring forth, and where conditions for a new way of communication can come to life.

I knew that I must create a project stemming from my vision. It was a force beyond me. I was just a vehicle. I felt myself to be part of a gigantic thread connecting surviving cultures, spiritual awareness, historical and racial wounds, sacrificial offerings, ecological consciousness, reawakening of the female energy, the encounter of the opposites—black and white, masculine and feminine, without beginning or end.

At this point I began to see the picture of this project more clearly. "Black and White Women Building a Bridge" was the title selected.

This multimedia project would include a series of workshops, a requisite for all women artists who wanted to be part of it. That would provide a sacred and safe place where African-Americans and European-Americans could have the opportunity to know each other. There would also be an art exhibit, with performances of music, songs and poetry. Finally, there would be a ceremony for "healing the wound between the races."

I was almost sure this could be done, but when? It was a big project. I went to Mexico and became immersed in preparations for the 500-year anniversary. That is when I saw the whole picture, the other half of the title. "Five hundred years in the land of the Native American." This put everything in perspective, because 500 years ago was the beginning of the contradictions that we are working to heal today.

Noris Binet

This painting was born of a vision, an image that exploded in my mind as Noris first spoke to me about "Black and White: Building a Bridge." It symbolizes reconciliation and a new beginning as these two women, one black and one white, eliminate old barriers and meet each other on a bridge they are building from heart to heart. Since as a child I was basically a "cartoon-head" and coloring-book connoisseur, color plays an important role in my art. Color has an incredible power. As with its origin, light, color can permeate or influence whatever it hits. Through the use of thick paint and bold color, I am able to express my views in a positive, humorous manner. I often use a tongue-in-cheek approach, because a sense of humor plays such a vital role in our lives, especially during these unusual times.

Bridge of Hearts
acrylic on canvas
36" x 48"

Renee LaRose

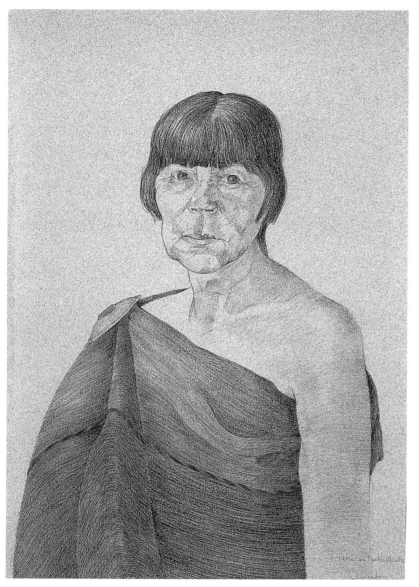

Gerri Tribe Ojibwa
charcoal/mixed media
30" x 24"

Flight

For I have seen your other face—
the dark side of your heart.
That pale and bloated sucker of your spirit
bargain with your freedom; buying it with lies

I have seen your pleading eyes
begging me to buy and go away.
Well, I'm seeing
but I ain't buying.

So I turn my face to seek the sun.
We will wait together
the bumbleweeds bare bones
and I.

We wait.
Our thorny arms open to embrace an empty room.
Those arms which held no welcome . . .
frozen in ghostly gesture.

Waken now and gaze in wonder
at this one who splits and shatters;
Raining seed with every blow.
Crumble to dust that brittle embrace.

To dance on the wind
and blossom in the morning mist.
In these shall be your memory.
In these shall I build my house.

House made of hope.

Minisa Crumbo

The

Voice

of a

Native

American

Let me begin by saying, my sisters and my brothers, that my soul seed lies rooted in the White Roots of Peace and manifests through the Sacred Flowering Tree.

I am Minisa Crumbo Halsey. I am of the Muskogee Creek and Pottawatomi tribes, German, French and Irish. Our family has been intermarried for many generations and my development has drawn, at one time or another, on all of these influences.

I was apprenticed to Bear Heart, a Medicine Man of the Muskogee Creek tribe of Oklahoma. Through this training, my personal endeavors and work in the world have been directed toward communicating traditional women's ways in the context of The Moon Circle Group gatherings for both women and men of all races and ages.

I am honored to speak of my heart's desires and concerns at this time. Women on the Inner Journey offers us, as women, a unique and rare opportunity to make an active contribution, through art, toward revealing ourselves in truth. For all true knowledge comes through the heart. And our hearts speak of many things: anguish and agony as well as joy and harmony, freedom and movement as well as bondage and limitation, friendship and love as well as enmity and alienation, unity as well as isolation.

We speak of the human condition in order to exorcise the demons of history, clear and illuminate the paths of reconciliation, and find ways that the people might live in harmony.

We all come crying for a vision, that we might truly forge the bridges necessary to move forward in a good way. Our lives depend on it. Our world depends on it.

For the old people have said: It is our prayers as well as our works that keep our world going. Let us remember that our world was created in beauty, and still is.

We thank you, Creator, for the opportunity to labor in your fields.

M'do,
Minisa Crumbo Halsey

Minisa Crumbo

Three

Feathers

I, a woman on an inner journey, am what the Cherokee call "Three Feathers," a mixture of races. My blood runs black, red and white. I am also a native Nashvillian whose ancestors have lived in Tennessee it seems like forever.

In my home and at church I learned racial and religious tolerance. But I grew up in a conservative WASP southern society which was severely segregated, a society that did not know about my racial origins. In college in North Carolina I met two people who became lifelong friends and helped me understand the problems and obstacles of racial prejudice. Much has been accomplished in the thirty years since we marched together for civil rights, but what remains is for us to take the ideals of freedom and equality and put them into action, for they are not just ideals, but basic truths.

We are all the same organism, the same basic human being that bleeds, excretes, eats, sleeps, knows joy and suffering, and dies when it is time. Only the decoration is different. It is now time for all who care to come together. The more we know and experience others of any race or culture, the more we understand them, and can act in harmony and sympathy for the betterment of all humanity.

In Nashville at this time there is not as much overt racial hatred as there is in other cities, but the lines of communication and channels of interaction (the bridges) are few. Even in avant-garde artistic circles, there is little mingling or socialization. Thus, in this culture, there is little chance of coming to personal knowledge and understanding among the races, including the newly arrived Asians.

A bridge is exactly what is needed now. A bridge is a form that allows each person to cross over into "another land," to explore and share commonalities; a structure that, once built, will allow others to follow. This is why I am involved in Women on the Inner Journey: Black and White Building a Bridge. I feel grateful to be able to use my skills and resources to help document this journey of women artists who have a vision of a society where there is no racial shame or blame. Experiencing the process (in the workshop) was transforming and brought me a realization about my personal power and the power of "coming together" for the common good.

My hope for the future of Nashville is that these seeds, the intent of this process, will find fertile ground and blossom into a human garden of rainbow colors, enriching our culture with the beauty of all our talents.

Joan French

A rt is a transformative tool which affords the opportunity to explore that which is highest and deepest within.

Sisterhood
acrylic on canvas
21" x 24"

The blood of all
Runs through me
African, Native American and most
Assuredly yours,
I am the true "All American". . .

Pat Smith

The Color of Blood

When you take a moment to consider all the injustice, the rape, the murder, the enslavement, the torture, the despair, the disrespect . . . all because of color, when will you finally become angry enough to see red?

My four-generational bloodline is mixed of Tribal African, European, Cherokee and Blackfoot as far as I know. The color of my skin is butterscotch, my eyes are brown, my hair is auburn black and thick and wiry. The color of my blood is red.

I do not know which tribe of Africa my family descends from. It has been suggested to me by a Senegalese man I met once in my travels in Paris that my features are similar to that of an Angolan. That is the closest I have come to tracing my African ancestry.

I am just as uncertain of my ancestral ties to Europe. I remember sitting on my grandfather's lap, on my father's side, and thinking he was a white man. All I know of my great–grandfather is a picture which hangs on a wall in the house of my aunt. It is of a very light complexioned man with fine features and straight hair. Besides that, and that our last name is British, before he died in 1987, my father asserted that we also have "some Irish blood in our veins." I know little else of the mixing of the races on my father's side of the family.

Besides that which is obvious by my physical appearance, the only familial roots I am absolutely certain of are Native American. I've only heard tales of some Cherokee men who took a few women in the family as wives. But I knew Grandma Owens, my great-grandmother on my mother's side. She lived to see 100 years come and go and for a long time after. She lived long enough for me to get to know her for her last and my first 13 years. She never talked much but she smiled a lot and loved family holidays. She'd been known for being pretty "lively" at the annual family New Year's Eve parties. What I remember best are the lines in her smooth brown face, her impeccable cheekbones and her thick long white braid. She looked pure Blackfoot squaw. She was beautiful, lived long and died peacefully.

She lives on in me.

I was born "whiter than all the white babies in the hospital," according to my mother, with thick curly blonde hair. That brief appearance of a European genetic influence receded early as my African and Native American genes became dominant. I see the red in my skin color and my thick hair and then I see my Grandma Owens. However, when I look at my nose, my lips, my thighs and my "back," I am certain I am also a descendant of African royalty.

Nevertheless, my blood is still red. I know that this is true because I bleed monthly. Just as an English, an Irish, a Cherokee, a Blackfoot, an Angolan, a Cayugan, a Celt, a Finn, a Norwegian, an Italian, a Spaniard, a Dane, a Haitian, an Austrian, a German, a Peruvian, a Colombian, a Tibetan, a Chinese, a Burmese, a Vietnamese, a Filipino, a Costa Rican, a Puerto Rican, a Dominican, a Jamaican, a Cuban, a Mayan, a Belgian, a Swede, a Russian, a Pole, a Ghanian, a Portuguese, a French Guyanese, an Arcadian, an Australian, an Eskimo, a Moroccan, a Somalian, a Samoan, a Kenyan, a Tunisian, a Bahian, a South African, an East Indian, a Palestinian, an Israeli, a Kuwaiti, a Saudi Arabian, an Eritrean, an Ethiopian, a Liberian, a Senegalese, a Thai, a Japanese, a Balinese, a Muslim, a Catholic, a Lutheran, a Quaker, a Baptist, a Mormon, a Hindu, a Buddhist or a Jewish woman bleeds monthly. We are all of the same blood.

I am every woman. Every man would not exist if not for me. Every man is of the same blood. Its color is red.

A blood transfusion that saves your life has no skin color. It does not racially discriminate. The red blood of life courses through the veins of every man, woman and child in every society, every culture and every race of human life on this planet. If it would save your life, you would not care if it came from a Croatian, a Jew, a Masai or a Bantu. You would welcome it. It would become part of you.

Because if you were to reject it, you would surely die. Just as, should you embrace it, you will surely live.

MaryAnne Howland

The

Opening

I shyly search the faces, looking for new friends,
wanting to reach out, tear time away,
clean the karma of the past.
I thank the Creator
when I hear the songs,
and know
fear won't last
if we do
as we are
doing now,
speaking,
touching,
singing,
dancing,
recognizing
We are One.
We come together
from many places,
different races, shades and hues,
a rainbow body of souls is formed,
a bridge to the heavens, after the summer storm.

Joan French

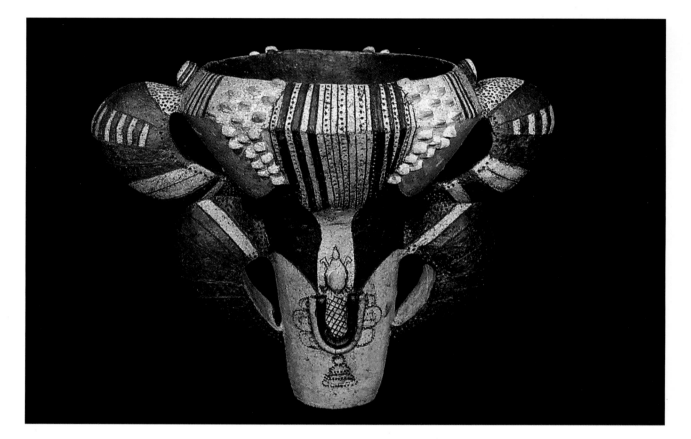

Ceremonial Bowl
clay

I follow the traditional African religions in their belief that God creates all our materials, therefore the craftsmakers create beauty in all their functional and ceremonial objects. My work is strongly influenced by those beautiful, spiritual, forceful images found in objects used in traditional African religious and cultural ceremonies. I enjoy the simple qualities of clay and natural fibers, both materials that at one time supported life. My objects are a celebration of life, and a conscious effort to balance myself with nature.

Viola Wood

A Society in Fragments

We are a society in fragments. If once we believed ourselves one nation, indivisible, now we define ourselves in terms of what separates us from one another.

Sex, race and economics are our major and most destructive divisions. Our society—"The System"—determines an individual's worth based on whether that person is male or female, white or black (or brown or yellow or red), rich or poor or somewhere in between. The most valuable, and therefore the most powerful, credible person in America is, and always has been, the wealthy, white male. Everyone else is worth less.

Certainly there are many other criteria for measuring personal worth, including physical appearance, age, education, sexual orientation and employment, but it is the big three that shape our lives most profoundly.

From the moment of birth, possibly sooner, we absorb spoken and unspoken messages from the world around us regarding our relative worth as human beings. These internalized value judgements affect our behavior, our emotions, the choices we make, the possibilities we see for ourselves, how we perceive ourselves and others, and our own self-worth. The further we are from being a wealthy white male, the more negative the messages are. The further we are from being a wealthy white male, the less responsive society is to our needs. So deep and subtle is this dynamic that few of us are even aware that it exists.

Regardless of race or economic status, all of us born female get the message that we are second-class citizens, less worthy, somehow, than persons born male. For generations untold we've lived with this lie, in part because to do otherwise would threaten our survival. Here, briefly, are just some of the reasons why.

Historical evidence, much of it revealed by modern technology, tells us that for thousands of years, men and women lived and worked side by side, in balance and harmony with each other and with Mother Earth. Their lives were determined by the rhythms of the seasons and the perpetual cycle of planting and harvesting. Ritual and ceremony honoring Mother Earth and expressing gratitude for her abundance were woven into the fabric of daily life. Archeological remains of some communities lack fortifications, indicating the people had no need to protect themselves from aggressors, from those who sought power over others. Women were healers, artisans, farmers, domesticators of animals, worshiped and revered for their unique ability to bring forth life.

All that began to change with the dawning of the Golden Age of Greece. Wholeness, balance and harmony gave way to patriarchy. The growing dominance of male over female accelerated in Europe during the Middle Ages, when, in the space of a few hundred years, possibly as many as nine million women were tortured and burned at the stake for practicing "witchcraft." The sin of witchcraft included practicing the healing arts and midwifery, accepted natural expressions of female energy since time out of mind.

Whatever balance may have remained began to vanish in 1770 with the onset of the Industrial Revolution. As the Western world moved from an agrarian to a manufacturing society, women relinquished their last contact with Mother Earth and Her ways, migrated to urban areas and went to work in shops and factories owned and run by men. Our modern age of science and high technology is simply the latest step on the journey away from wholeness toward the fragmented world in which we live today.

Mathematics, science, logic, analysis and separation are aspects of masculine energy. Art, music, perceptions of patterns and systems, and connection are aspects of feminine energy. Together in equal proportions, the two energy forces compliment and complete each other, creating a perfectly balanced whole. The extreme fragmentation we are now experiencing, in America and around the world, is a cancer-like result of our loss of balance, a potentially fatal manifestation of male energy out of control. Even Mother Earth, who nurtures and supports us all, has been so brutally raped and battered that She may be unable to survive.

These thousands of years of male domination have taken an incredible toll on women. We have suppressed, denied and become estranged from those aspects of our distinctly female selves that threaten or challenge men, because our survival has depended, quite literally, on gaining and keeping their favor. So deeply have we absorbed the illusion of our own inferiority, and men's superiority, that we have become partners with men in maintaining the illusion. Even the Women's Liberation movement, which has accomplished a great deal on many fronts, has done so by organizing women to act out of their male energy. In our effort to gain equality we have become, in effect, men. But it is those who were born male who still control the majority of money and power, and effectively limit our access to either. Our anger and pain continue to grow.

When aspects of our intuitive female essence force themselves into our consciousness we are suspicious, afraid, ready to call ourselves crazy, to deny our truth. Alienated from our authentic selves, we have become by extension alienated from our sisters. What we cannot value in ourselves, we judge to be even more worthless in other women. We act out our feelings of powerlessness against our sisters in countless hurtful, separating

Penny Case

ways. Nowhere is this alienation more evident than between white women and women of other races. The cynical quip: if we can't feel good about ourselves, at least we can feel we're better than somebody else.

Although men appear to fare better than women in our world, they, too, are deeply wounded, and it is merely an illusion that they are in control. The reality is that this unbalanced male energy has careened wildly beyond their command. It is no longer a question of who will rule whom. The question now is will we explode from within, burn in the fires of our own rage, drown in our own entropy, or perish with our planet when She dies?

Or do we women have the power to make a different choice?

The Chinese character for "crisis" embodies the dual concepts of danger and opportunity. Yes, we are in a time of great crisis. This crisis cannot be solved with more guns or bombs or laws or oppression or economic manipulation. But we pioneers, we artists, we women on the inner journey, have at this moment of clear and present danger an unprecedented opportunity to change the course of history and begin to heal our world.

The starting point is, as always, with ourselves. As passionate travelers on our inner journey, we will sooner or later discover our essence, the source of our creativity, that place within us of unlimited, authentic power. We will recognize on a profoundly deep level a rich, multifaceted part of ourselves which is connected to and is the same in all women. Once that recognition occurs, a healing transformation has begun. We become able to love and accept first ourselves, then others. We then can take the second step: bridging the gap that separates us from our sisters, embracing that which makes us one.

Our first connection outside ourselves is likely to be with other artists on the inner journey, like-hearted women with whom we can exchange support. For our own healing and the healing of the world, it is vitally important that we extend this connection to include our artist sisters of all races. Sometimes women of different races will reach out to each other simultaneously. When that does not occur, those of us who are white must reach out first, because we have been, and are, the oppressors of people of color. Both as individuals and as a group we can share our personal and mutual healing with the others by sharing our art—painting, sculpture, poetry, dance, music, stories, crafts, photography, theater—whatever we create. This is the traditional role of the artist.

But we are also women, and it is a traditional role of women to be healers in the community. The role of woman-as-healer can be created in many ways.

With only a few of us, black and white together, we can take our healing work into the community. We could choose to start by reaching out to our sisters who are homeless; our sisters on welfare; our sisters who, though still children themselves, are having their own babies in order to have someone to love them; to our sisters who are helpless and hopeless and powerless to change their lives. We can use what we're learning about art and ritual and the inner journey to help them discover a sense of their own worth, to help our sisters find their inner beauty and power, to help them create the personal tools to make a better life.

With only a few of us, black and white together, we can reach out to our disenfranchised children, those who are poverty-stricken, homeless, fatherless, motherless, hungry; those whose lives are filled with desperation, violence and despair. We can use what we know to give them experiences of creating something good—a picture, a song, a puppet, a story—that comes from inside themselves. For most of these children, this would be their first time to experience themselves as worthy, possibly valuable beings.

With only a few of us, black and white together, we can find a multitude of ways to manifest our creative female energy in our most oppressed and alienated communities. We can support our sisters and their families in regenerating racial and ethnic pride, in renewing and creating tradition and ritual, in bringing generations back together. We can offer our female energy as a power source for the creation of community vegetable and flower gardens, neighborhood beautification projects, nurturing care for children, for the sick, for the elderly, and so much more.

Perhaps we can even, black and white together, in a totally female and artistic way, create a ritual for the healing of our deepest wounds, those inflicted by slavery, oppression, sexism and racism. Perhaps we pioneers, we artists, we women on the inner journey can connect with each other from our deepest, most loving selves to bring light to our darkest demons. Perhaps we can combine all we create . . . music, painting, chanting, dance, theater, ceremony—into a powerful ritual in which we confront our collective shadow and all its surrounding pain, own it, then destroy it so completely it can never rise up against us again.

Yes, we humans are a society in fragments, a world in crisis. But the danger need not be fatal if we women on the inner journey reconnect with ourselves and our sisters soon, then embrace this opportunity to manifest our authentic, nurturing, balancing female energy in our outer world. Healing is our thrilling journey. Wholeness can be our joyful destination.

Penny Case

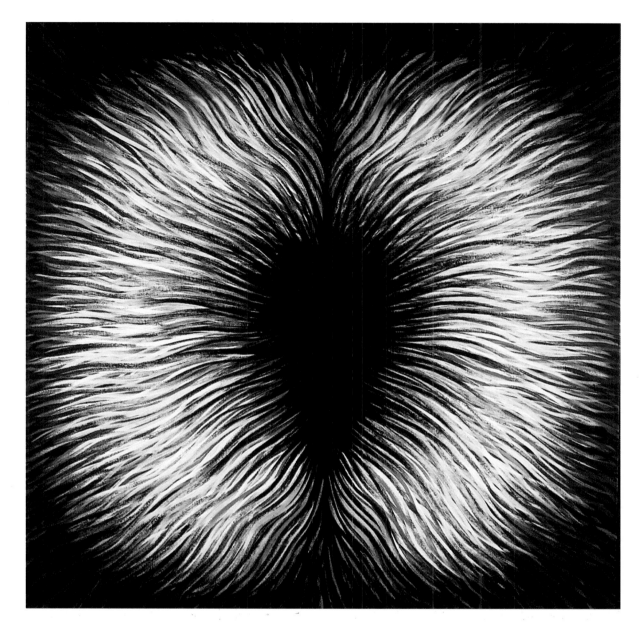

A-11
acrylic image
65" x 65"

I am reaching beyond myself to try to capture the substructure behind reality—the stuff of which we are made. Most of my pieces deal with duality in both form and color: light-dark, red-blue, I-thou, microcosm-macrocosm. They chronicle my emergence from a dark and painful passage, through which I came to celebrate the immense strength and creative source within and beyond, that which we are and that which surrounds us. Although I think of shapes, colors, patterns, and rhythms, they are not the issue. I paint who I am—and now—I paint my genesis.

Jane Braddock

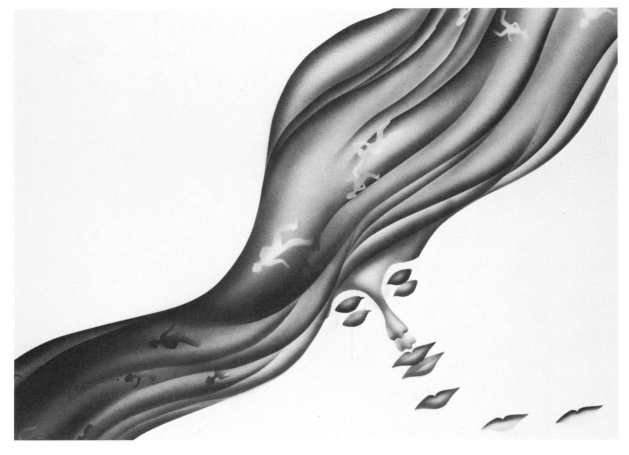

Women on the Inner Journey
ink on paper

Noris Binet

Women on the Inner Journey

We are on the edge of a new era, a new species, a new time.
We are on the edge of the unknown, of the darkness and the light.
Slowly and precariously, we walk the fine line. Too much to the
right or too much to the left can make us fall.
On our backs we carry our dreams.
Women gather to express part of their particular journey
from a deep necessity of sharing, nourishing, supporting.
From time immemorial, women and men have gathered in their own groups,
understanding their separate identities.

Why Women?
Women are the matrix where new life is born and grows.
That is why women have a very particular mission in finding an understanding of
being,
of being on the edge of a new era, a new species. We pass through a similar experience
when a new baby is brought to life, to light.

Walking on the edge of the unknown,
We need to be able to find the center, to be in the center,
to keep the center, and finally, to be the center.
This is why we share with the community what we see and how we see,
from the fine line we are walking between today and tomorrow.

Why Women?
Because we are the earth in which new life is born:
women who are traveling on their inner journey
bring back to consciousness images, visions, and insights
which must be exposed to the light
for society to find its awareness, its understanding.
Because the first art was not a mastery of color and form
to hang from the walls of the caverns.
Art, from the beginning, was the deep communications of the human soul
with the Great Source from which we come.
Art is a sacred act, not a decoration piece.
It is the power of the cosmic energy,
concentrated in a symbol where we can find nourishment.

Noris Binet

Making

the

Inner

Journey

"Let's Plant a Seed in Your Heart"

Looking back at what happened in the workshop, the phrase "planting a seed in your heart" kept coming to me. The heart, a very ancient symbol, began coming to me over the last few years as I was trying to find my center. Since then, it is the most important image to emerge and reemerge in my work. Each time the heart symbol appears, it brings a new energy, a new power which provokes in me a profound fascination.

In the process of our several workshops, many hearts opened themselves and allowed the new seed to be implanted.

The workshop is the real core of this whole project, because it is where the work of digging into the earth of our limitations and potentials starts. It is where we create a sacred place in which our transformative energy can be contained.

We try to avoid our limitations and blockages, to fight them. We keep ourselves in tremendous inner battles. Instead, we should stop and look closely at our blockages. We will find garbage, pain, anger, sadness, guilt, etc. It has always been there, but we were unable to see. The great surprise is that, when we repress painful feelings, we repress joyful feelings, too. The beautiful thing to see is that sometimes we cry and cry until we start laughing, and we can feel that a big liberation has happened.

From this perspective I decided that the goal of this workshop was to create the conditions in which each participant would be able to get in touch with herself, with her emotions, journeying toward her center, the center where we are One with creation and the creator. Only from this place can forgiveness be born and healing exist.

This initial workshop was planned a couple of months in advance to coincide with the new moon of May, 1992. An interesting act of synchronicity occurred that week with the Rodney King verdict, and the subsequent riots in Los Angeles and thirteen other cities. Several women called, wondering if African Americans would come to the workshop. These were questions that I could not answer. The only thing in my mind was that if we were working on the side of the spirit, the spirit would take care and everything would happen in the proper way.

When the morning arrived and with it our time to meet, the black and white women who were supposed to be there were there, and the spirit was with us one more time.

This synchronicity confirmed in my mind that the time was ripe, that this was the right direction.

We started the morning sitting around an altar that was a floor mandala invoking the mother ocean. She represents the beginning of life. This mandala was composed of shells and candles pointing to the four directions. The four directions symbolize the earth and women. Somebody brought a little blooming plant that we put in the center to represent new life.

We all became centered in silence, to find a place inside ourselves where we could be comfortable and relax, a place where we could trust and be in peace. From this place we introduced ourselves to each other, then prayed together for the Divinity to assist us with its presence and guide our efforts toward whatever direction we needed to go.

I would like to be very clear that the real focus of this project was healing, which can only happen from the spiritual plane. I used different techniques to help each individual to have access to the part of herself which might open to a broader perspective. The goal was to enable each one to feel free to laugh, cry, dance, fear and have the courage to explore new possibilities: a human being encountering her own limitations and her own pain, a woman finding her vulnerability and strength with other women. In order to do this, each had to enter a space where the hold of the logical world could be broken. Each had to give birth to the illogical, the unexpected, the dream, the fantasy, the hope of transformation.

It is not easy for a black woman to forgive the humiliation and the mutilation that her race has been subjected to, the tragic reality that she is judged to be less because of the color of her skin, and that she has to fight daily to overcome a world of oppression.

Neither is it easy to ask a white woman to be close to a black woman, to open the door of communication and receive whatever may come through it. This door has been closed for so long that guilt, fear, shame and rage are just a few of the things that will probably come through that door before they learn to trust each other.

My work is focused in the body, because I think that it is on the physical level that our humanity begins. Using movement and dance, with certain kinds of music and sensitive guidance, people are able to get in touch with themselves and, from there, get in touch with others. Going more and more into the body, we are less and less in the mind. This process utilizes many different rhythms, exercises, games, and interrelations between individuals until the group becomes comfortable together.

At this point people are usually very energetic and alive because of the increased amount of oxygen in their bodies, which increases their metabolism. This is a good moment for them to have a break, or possibly lunch, to give people an opportunity to contact each other in the context of what they have been discovering about themselves.

In this first workshop, when we came back from lunch we went to the altar and talked about our inner experiences. We started to touch the connection that some of them had made with their own feelings, from a personal level to a social level. The anger that many felt about what was happening in Los Angeles came to the surface.

From here the remaining question was "What can we do to help transform the pain into consciousness?"

This was basically a group of artists, not only visual artists but writers, songwriters, poets and musicians as well. Here was the opportunity for us to start to understand things from another perspective—art. Art is a medium in which individuals have the ability to open themselves, to receive not only the content of their individual unconscious, but also the potential to connect with the collective unconscious that belongs to the whole human race.

Keeping in touch with all these feelings, we came back into the body with energetic movements to tap into these emotions. Then we began to draw on a piece of white paper using only black charcoal.

We explored how to keep the feelings flowing onto the paper. I used a particular music for maintaining the rhythm of these emotions. When everybody finished, we came back into a circle, putting our artwork on the floor. Then we explored again, with movement, the interconnection between our work and our bodies.

The goal of this part of the process was to merge with our own creations and, through movement, bring an understanding of these images and symbols to our whole system. We finished with a thankful prayer. At this point we were ready to close the day, with great release and great bonding among us.

The next day I felt the group was ready to continue exploring their abilities to create individual sacred space. With lighted candles provided for each one, they were to focus their energy on healing through meditation and prayer.

Each participant selected a quiet spot in the room where she was comfortable and private, taking her artwork from the day before and bringing back the emotional connections in order to travel on her individual journey. At the same time, she was connected with her brothers and sisters in other cities who were passing through tremendous suffering.

Some of the women found themselves very open and vulnerable. Tears came to some as they prayed. At this point they were able to support each other—beyond their skin color, they were just women. The personal pain and the social pain became one, and they were free to expose their deepest feelings in each other's company.

When everybody was ready, we came together around the Mandala and integrated our individual experiences with those of the whole group. This was a very empowering act. Each one had a very particular journey to tell about, and laughter and tears intermingled.

Each one talked about the meaning of her work. One African American woman's image was "a woman on the top of a mountain standing alone." Her story was about her great-grandmother who was forced to abandon her village because her husband was accused of sleeping with a white woman. She took her five children and left and never saw her home again. This story, told by the great-grandchild, was very powerful. It made everybody cry in a cathartic way, because the whole group shared the same emotion. The experience helped us to see the larger picture of our work, beyond our present time and space.

I offer this example of one of the workshops to help in understanding how this work was done. That does not mean this is the only way it can be done; every group is different, and every community as well. I think it is very important to adjust the work to the demands and characteristics of the community.

Actually, my workshops with groups that included men have been substantially different, although they shared the same goal of building bridges between black and white.

There are many dimensions to this kind of work. Maybe you are asking "But how is healing to happen, and how will it have an effect on the prejudices of society?" There is no clear answer. It can only be said that it happens. As my great-aunt would say, "The spirits are making their works." Ultimately there is no separation between mind and body, or between individuals and society; we are whole.

I was able to learn many things in this process. One of them is that when African Americans are able to be with a group of white people who treat them as equals and value them for who they are, the pressures relax, and the relaxation is there for both. For white people who are ready to make this step, there is a great opportunity to be released from their feelings of guilt.

This workshop, happening in a time of social unrest, made all these women feel that they were able to do something, that at least a group of women in Nashville had the courage to get together and create a healing space bringing a new understanding. They experienced that they were not helpless and without hope, there were things that could be done. For some, that was the beginning of a new way.

Noris Binet

Since 1985 I have been involved in Sacred Circle Dance, and in the past five years teaching this spiritual dance has become my focus. Something profound happened to me when I began attending Circle Dance. My awareness of who I am and others around me exploded.

The Spiral Dance of Life
ink
24" x 30"

Heather Thompson

Woman

to

Woman

since the first black woman
was brought to this land
we have been intimately familiar
with our white sisters
we have been exposed to every detail
of your existence
we have washed your drawers
cooked your food
nursed you & your family when you were sick
nursed your babies when you were too
    weak & delicate to feed them yourselves
nursed them from our own black breasts
    that your brother, father, or husband later laid his whip
              across
we have seen you in your fine underwear
    & we have watched your creamy white skin
           shrivel up in the sun
we have seen your men treat you like
    fragile porcelain dolls
& then come to us to demonstrate
        how they really feel about women
we have lost our men to your totemic "beauty"
& we have tried to make ourselves look like you
    to get them back
& after all of this
you do not even have a clue
you do not know who we are
    or who you are yourselves
you are lost
as are we all
unless we
ourselves
find
our sister selves
within our common
ancestral
womb
& give birth
to the new
world

Gwynelle Dismukes

The
Crone

Wrinkles
    soft lines caressing her face
    lines of wisdom
    lines of knowledge
gentle eyes
    seeing all
    taking her sight into a deep knowing
    heart of gentleness
    voice
        not loud, not soft
        not wordy
            but imparting deep wisdom with every word
presence
    you know she has always been there
    she is beyond time and place
    yet she knows time and place
she sees and feels the scars
    but they no longer weigh her down
    she has attained the deeper knowing
    that only she and those like her have attained
yet she is willing to see
    feel
    care
    for me
a tender, yet strong and sure gift she gives in herself
    she comes to me—she sees me.

I am aware of her dance
    external
    internal
no quick sudden movements
    slow
    sure
the dance of life
the dance of death
she is not afraid
she dances on

I begin to dance
    timidly
        meekly
            afraid
she takes my hand and gently pulls me into the ring
she leads
I follow
    falling into the rhythm
        falling into my body
I follow on and on as she leads

Angela Smith

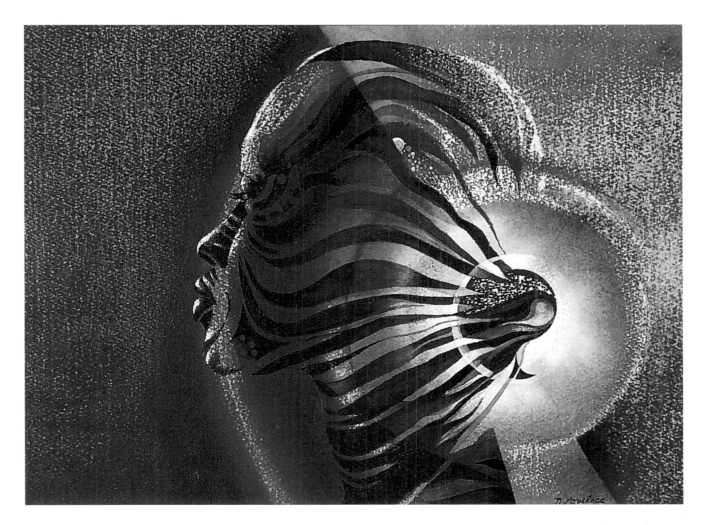

Soular Eclipse
watercolor
16" x 21"

Years ago in a course on African art our professor, David Driskell, introduced us to writers who spoke of art as not essentially an object, but as an active vital force and a way of being and doing. My views about art were greatly affected. I can recall spending hours looking at the numerous original African sculptures which were among the collection now named in honor of Aaron Douglas at Fisk University. I was fascinated not only by the forms and designs of those magnificent works, but also by their power. In many of those, I was struck by the quality that has been described as being in perfect balance and repose, yet simultaneously so potent with dynamic power. Historian Robert F. Thompson has related such qualities to a profound moral wisdom—the ability to move and act with collectedness of mind in the midst of change—which he informs us is a statement of character at the highest level. I wish through my paintings to emulate that kind of wisdom, to generate that quality of energy.

Nina Lovelace

All the Difference between Dark & Light
oil
50" x 40"

Because of my race, which is easily spotted, not understood and generally scorned, I have not been innocent since I was three. White girls are innocent. They are the precious ones— the pretty ones that everyone likes and takes care of. Everything is a conflict to me. I have a thousand unanswered questions and must make a thousand changes for every situation. I become hard and worldly before I am out of grammar school. They remain naive. That naivete still makes me angry. Sometimes I wish I had that luxury of just being a girl. I would like to snatch that innocence and naivete away. So much of my life has been taken away being a "race." Sometimes I would like to know what it is like just being a woman.

Barbara Bullock

Both Sides of the Veil

Last February, prior to the opening of the Women on the Inner Journey exhibit, America went to war in the Persian Gulf. This act gave an added dimension to our exhibit in the form of prayers for peace which were placed by the public on our altar, and it brought into sharper focus the need for women artists to exert their influence on a troubled world.

This April, only days before our workshop, "Black & White: Building A Bridge," America was rocked by violent civil disturbance, a result of racial injustice. The environment in which we undertake our work lends a dramatic sense of urgency to our peace-making mission, and calls us to respond, both internally and externally, to a profound moral, artistic and spiritual challenge.

We are to "create a space in which to break through the barriers between black and white, and open the door through which our individualities dissolve." Yet for me it took the riots in Los Angeles to bring clearly into focus what it is that needs to happen. Only now do I see what it is that has been happening all along.

Among African Americans, one of the most volatile, and most infuriating statements made by European Americans is "I don't see color, I just see human beings." European Americans are usually baffled by the strong reaction this gets from otherwise accommodating black people. I, myself, have never fully understood my own gut revulsion to this expression. I could intellectually, morally, psychologically defend it, but I could never really identify what it was in the depths of my being that reacted with such strong aversion to hearing this. I realize now the reason for my confusion and the problem that is so much deeper than skin.

To "not see color" is such a well-intentioned sentiment on the part of those who profess it, but 99 percent of the time, it simply is not true. European Americans assert it as truth, and will not accept it as their own illusion; people of color know it is not true because we are already there and we can see that they are not there with us. What European Americans fail to realize is that it is possible to be "without color" only at the very deepest level of our being; to "see everyone as the same" can occur only at that same level. This is the level of spirit, it is the experience of the soul. It can be accessed only through a spiritual encounter with the total self. In our modern society it is impossible to live and act on this level at all times, or even most of the time. Therefore, it is impossible not, at some time, to see color. To say "I only see human beings," without qualifying it in some way, is simply telling a lie.

African Americans are well versed in dealing on more than one level because of the dual-consciousness we have developed in response to our systematic, historical and continuing oppression in this country. We know who we are as a people and we have a deep understanding of European Americans that is intensified by the nature of our relationship to them.

European Americans, on the other hand, in ignorance or denial of that relationship, are removed from any true understanding of black people as human beings, and so are able to relate to them for the most part only on surface levels. Black people know and understand this, and so we are always compensating, always changing levels in order to make some kind of co-existence possible. This flexibility of consciousness has been key to our survival in a hostile environment, while the spiritual development of European Americans has been buried under layers of deception, delusion and institutional domination.

It is no wonder that European Americans are now having trouble "getting in touch with themselves," are suffering from feelings of alienation and loss. Any armchair psychologist would know that you cannot spend your entire life ignoring someone with whom you have the most intimate relationship, someone you have been living with every day, someone who is indispensable to you, except at the expense of your mental and emotional health. Let us consider then, that this has been going on for generations, and we have an idea of the collective psychic imbalance that European Americans are currently experiencing.

The kind of damage that has been done to both blacks and whites can only be repaired in those deep levels where the imprint of our common anger, pain and grief remain alive. We must awaken ancestral ghosts and bury them again, finally and decently. We must re-open fatal wounds and let them bleed again, and together rescue ourselves from our own near death. We must take on all the guilt, the fear, the hatred, the confusion, the trauma and allow ourselves to be utterly consumed by them until some part of ourselves dies and all that we have all suffered dies along with it.

Then, there will be nothing left, except for us to be reborn.

We women are especially familiar with the process of birth. Even if a woman has no children, she is bound by biological rhythms to the act of creation. The whole feminine aspect of being involves the continual renewal of spring, cycles of sowing and harvesting, new life, and rebirth. Women by nature should be more effective and less damaged in breaking through the blockages that are part of rebirth.

On another level, we recognize that, as women, we are confronted by common issues that transcend race, religion, nationality—crucial issues that have to do with the preservation of our lives and the lives of our children. At some level we must collectively view ourselves as the archetypal "Great Mother" who is responsible for all of humanity—and the planet—as her children.

Gwynelle Dismukes

"Any words of mine, however halting or eloquent, cannot reveal, indeed, can barely hint at the meanings locked in the works exposed here," wrote sculptor Leonard Baskin. This sentence eloquent in its simplicity, houses the very essence of the multilayered ideas that co-exist within my own images. My figuratively shaped landscape images stem from my personal response to the forms I see so vividly described in nature, in the overlapping leafless branches of the tree and the weather-carved solid forms of rocks. I enlarge these patterns and allow them to speak as symbols of other, less known environments that I call my inner-scapes. I want my viewers to feel a presence—the illusive spirit in us all, housed in nature's indefinable soul.

Wound
pastel on paper
19" x 28"

Dori Lemeh

Wound
pastel on paper
19" x 28"

I have always been an artist, always loved the process of making art. It is an important way for me to let my deepest Self speak, and to be aware of what Stephen Levine calls "our true spacious nature." Today our planet needs the best we can give, our most powerful, most realized selves. I want to respond to this imperative and am passionately interested in art's power to transform on a personal as well as a community level.

Jane Fleishman

Art and Dance Beyond the Ego

I came late to the workshop. As I entered the room, the blinds were drawn and I saw 14 women sitting on the floor around a blanket, the four corners of which were turned under to create an octagon shape. In the center was an earthen vase filled with purple irises, at each octagon point a flickering red or blue candle and four conch shells. A song was playing that Vanessa, one of the workshop participants, had written for the art exhibit. It was such a moving and powerful song that I got goosebumps on my arms and a chill ran up my spine. It was at that point that I knew I would learn and experience something special that day.

I found an opening in the circle and sat down. Each woman discussed her view of the L.A. incident (the riots following the Rodney King trial verdict). We all agreed it was sad to see people destroy their own neighborhood, but we empathized with them, too, since all of us had felt frustration upon hearing the "not guilty" verdict. Then each of us went into a deep meditation and focused on the anger, suffering, confusion and bewilderment the people in Los Angeles were experiencing. We put ourselves in the shoes of a mother whose child died during the riots, of people whose businesses were burned down, of gang members who already saw their future as hopeless, and were once more frustrated by a judicial system they felt was stacked against them, of whites pulled from their vehicles and beaten as scapegoats, of children watching their neighborhoods erupt into vandalism, riots and death.

We felt ALL of this! We focused these feelings into art with charcoal—each creating our fury on paper, in silence. You could feel the energy—each one of us creating our own riot on paper, black smudged fingers working frantically. As we each completed our work we took our pictures and placed them in a circle on the floor, then walked around them, viewing all of the artwork. Next, Noris guided us to dance in front of our own pictures—dancing away the anger and frustration. It was a beautiful sight to see all the writhing figures releasing the negative energy to make room for the positive. This process was very moving for me; it showed me how 15 of us could view the same incident and express it so differently with words and art, yet all come to the same awareness of oneness, sharing, caring, love, enlightenment and peace in the end. I believe that was our purpose, to raise our own consciousness so we could then help raise the consciousness of others.

I came away from the workshop knowing that our small circle of women helped to heal our planet. I know that our group will spread love and peace and goodwill. We each did our part generating positive energy. We will pass this on to our group of friends, they will pass it on to theirs, and on and on. It was good to know that I helped start something so beautiful, and good to have the opportunity to absorb the love and compassion we all shared with each other and share with the world and its people.

Lynda Bates

The elemental essence of art—as with life itself—is evolution. Our inner landscapes both bloom and erode as experience forms and shades them over time. My art is reflective of this process of growth: sometimes joyous, sometimes painful. Each work is a footprint on the long path of a spiritual journey, a capture of moments that reflect the struggles, the triumphs, the confusion and the certainties that confront all humankind.

Together We Stand
watercolor/mixed media
12" x 36"

Johnnie Enloe

Art and Dance Beyond the Ego

Saturday morning, early May. Great smoking flames of rage rolled out of the City of Angels and across America. Around the world, new incidents of racial and ethnic strife exploded like strings of firecrackers out of the still-hot ashes of political oppression.

In a second-floor room at Scarritt-Bennett Center, Nashville, Tennessee, we met. A gathering of women, friends and strangers, black, white, brown. Women of different life experiences, different ages. But all women. All creative. All somewhere on the inner journey, meeting this day with one intention: to explore ways of bridging the gaps between us. No one spoke of the fire outside, not at first, but it was there with us, fueling our desires to reach out to one another, to connect.

But what could we do, really? How could we create any significant change? The situation seemed hopeless, overwhelming. But what transpired in our time together during the next two days showed us possibilities that most of us had only dreamed.

We didn't discuss. We didn't analyze. We didn't brainstorm, or appoint committees. We engaged, instead, in process, actions and rituals which moved us out of thinking and into being.

We moved and danced in freeing new ways until our conscious awareness moved out of our heads, out of the numbness of thinkingthinkingthinking, out of limiting self consciousness, and into our bodies, our female bodies. The more we moved, the more alive, the more fully ourselves we became. Under the gentle guidance of Noris Binet, we went deeper into our bodies and began to experience our emotions— joy, sorrow, playfulness, tenderness and more. Using our eyes and our movements, we explored ways of communicating our feelings to one another, and soon had a sense that, in each of us, those feelings are the same.

As the process continued, at once communal and intensely personal, we went deeper, moving even further beyond thinking, beyond judgement, beyond shame, beyond ego and all the walls it builds between us. Far inside ourselves, traveling on our inner journey, searching for that place that is the same for all Creation, that place where thinking cannot go. When from time to time we gathered as a group, or paired off one on one, what we gave to and received from each other had an unaccustomed quality to it, as if it came from some rich place where grace and wisdom grow.

Not until we'd become aware of our connections to ourselves and each other did we invite the raging fire outside to formally come in. We said those few words that needed to be said, then, each in her own way, drew our pain and anger and grief and frustration with black charcoal on white paper. Our shadow art became a vehicle for further interior travel, taking us into feelings that might otherwise be too painful, too frightening to explore.

Sunday brought more process, more vulnerability, more light, more apparent willingness to feel our own, each other's and the world's pain. It was a morning for being sisters together; for simply accepting ourselves and each other; for examining what it truly is to be female; for embracing our newly found inner power; for honoring our Mother Earth; for celebrating our female energy; for hope; for creating a way for healing to begin.

Penny Case

In my work, I am trying to express the symbolic content of my inner process. The images emerging from that process create a magical world where I can explore other realities, where transformation and healing can happen. The more I experience that inner world, the more I find an interconnection between it and the colors, shapes and vibrations of the universe, as well as a connection to the natural laws that govern every living manifestation.

The birth of this piece was the energy that kept me going during the turbulent emotional moments of this project. Each symbol gave a new insight about myself and the whole process, becoming a map that I simultaneously followed and created.

Sacrificial Offering
ink pencil/mixed media
40" x 60"

Noris Binet

The

Opening

Celebration: The Whole

I mentioned earlier the need to create safe sacred space in which all races can share and start to know each other. We have been talking until this point about inner space, inner process. This is the first dimension, the one in which this group of women were creating a vessel to contain their healing energy for themselves and for the community. This is the great beauty of this kind of work, that we bring healing to others at the same time that we heal ourselves. The process of healing is a process of becoming one with "the inclusive love" of the great mother, the giver of life to everything without distinction, manifesting in her magnificent richness of colors and shapes what life is.

Now we are prepared for the second dimension, in which the unconscious and the conscious meet. This is a sacred act, because it is when wholeness can exist. In ancient time and in Native American culture today, this is a ceremony in which the whole community participates, because art and spirituality are not separate from their daily life, they are interwoven, forming a colorful tapestry of music, dance, garments, chants, food, symbols—a celebration of the sacred and the profane.

My initiation into these native cultures really changed my whole perception of art, helping me to not only reclaim, but accept the many facets of expression that exist in me and in every human being who can keep the connection with the primal source.

I worked from this view of wholeness in planning the opening of the exhibit at the gallery. First, I involved the artists in the whole event. They not only created their work to be exhibited, they also took responsibility for mailing invitations (some wrote notes on the invitations to make them more personal), helping with hanging the show, with promoting the event by putting flyers in their neighborhoods and churches. They carried information with them to give to people they met, not only to those who already have a particular interest in art, but to people who, just because their invitation was personal, might explore art for the first time and open a new avenue for themselves. The women also brought food and drink for the opening celebration, and were present to meet the public.

Part of the exhibit is an altar of symbols that will connect the public with the sacredness of the place, where members of the community can participate with their prayers and be an active part of the event.

The altar was done the day before the exhibit. I invited every participant to come for our last gathering in our private world. Each one talked about her work and through a ritual we made the place sacred to receive the public, the community. This is an act of love. It is when we become the generous host for the most holy guest. When we are in that space, we become spiritual servants, ready for being in unconditional love, sharing with everybody at any time. It is when we no longer belong to ourselves, but to the others. We become empty of ourselves and allow that emptiness to be filled with the energy of the others.

The gallery had become our matrix. During the opening ceremony, with the wall of our matrix sustaining our paintings, and the excitement of everybody, we moved into music, songs and poetry created for and from this particular process of black and white building bridges. This is our best opportunity to use the incredible power of music to build bridges among people. With everybody holding hands and singing together, many beautiful feelings came to the surface.

In this setting, the women who had been working with this music during the whole process reconnected with their inner landscapes and took the public with them.

This is a great gift, where we finally break the boundaries between the creator and the creation, the artists and the public. It is a moment when some realize that we are only servants, vehicles of the universal energy, in which all of us become one.

Noris Binet

Wholeness

Noris Binet

The Ceremony and Altar

I was involved in the creation of the altar only a short time before I realized that it was creating itself. Although Native American spirituality informs much of what I do spiritually, and composes much of what I am spiritually, I am not American Indian, and I do not attempt to practice or teach their traditions. It is, however, the spirituality of the people and of the land where we live. I have studied it and I respect it. My personal association to indigenous spirituality comes through my Celtic heritage, and that is the tradition I feel most legitimate practicing.

Before laying an altar, I sit in the space, becoming familiar with its shape and size, its relationship to the four directions, the lighting, the subtle energies of the place. I also become familiar with the intentions of the project or occasion for which it is being prepared. The altar should reflect the spirit of the project as well as focus it. I then consider the season of the year and the phase of the moon. Working with this information I begin to select the individual objects that will become the altar. Things to be considered are: shape, size, colors, texture, intention, function, clarity, integrity to purpose and, of course, beauty.

When Noris first asked me to prepare an altar, she told me the purpose of the project was Black and White Women Building a Bridge. As I began to prepare the altar, the images that came to me were Native American. I always honor the four directions, and work with the elements of air, fire, water and earth. However, this time they placed themselves on a background of red, yellow, black and white—traditional Native American colors. When I meditated on the center space which is the point of transformation, the Pipe appeared. Tobacco and prayer ties followed. It also came to me to place vigil lights on the altar for people to light—a Roman Catholic tradition, from the religion of the group who first conquered the "New Land."

I was not completely comfortable borrowing and mixing symbols, and working outside of my tradition, yet the altar was insisting I go in that direction. I called a friend of mine who is a Lakota Sioux to sound it out with him. He laughed and told me that I knew exactly what Spirit was telling me to do, and to do it! I called Noris and told her that the altar was becoming Native American. She said it was entirely appropriate as the full title of the project was: "Black and White Building a Bridge: 500 Years in the Land of the Native American"!

The Ceremony

Margaret Meigs had laid the altar the previous year and kept the candle. The ceremony opened by her presenting it to me. In this way we honored those who had come before us. We smudged with sage, and cast a circle—creating sacred time and space. We honored the four directions with the Prayer for Oneness. Great Spirit was invoked by each individual recognizing the God of her understanding. Each artist presented her work, telling about the process involved in creating it and in selecting it for the show. Noris spoke of our need to recognize the pain of the history we bring together in order to heal it. We came together as the oppressor, the slave and the conquered people. One of the items I had brought for the ceremony was a 20,000-year-old grinding stone called a Mono. The stone was given to me by relatives in Arizona and had been in the hands of women as they worked together grinding grain for many centuries. As we passed the stone around the circle each woman held it silently allowing it to speak to her, to impart healing. It was then placed on the altar in the north—the direction that honors the Mother Earth.

The Pipe was lit and passed around the circle. The Way of the Pipe means many things and is central to Native teachings. O Mitakuye Oyasin—To All My Relations—is a Native Prayer. As the Pipe returned to my hands I knew I needed to recognize my position as a white woman, as a guest in the Land of the Native American. I presented the Pipe to Noris, asking permission from her as a Native Woman, for me to live on her land. Noris accepted the Pipe as a Tainos of Anauak, the native people of the Dominican Republic. I acknowledged the destruction my race has brought through slavery and violence to her people. I renewed my pledge to work for the liberation of all people and the healing of the earth. This was a very powerful moment in the ritual for me as it has been difficult for me to find peace within myself as a member of the oppressing class. In that ceremony, I found forgiveness followed by peace.

The women placed personal items on the altar, made prayer ties and lighted vigil lights. An item of particular importance was a black doll one of the women had found in a secondhand store. It had been dressed in traditional slave wear. She took the doll home and made her an African costume, transforming her appearance. It was the presence of the transformed slave doll that was needed to complete the symbols on the altar.

The altar was central to the project, inviting participation. Noris speaks of the artist as magician. Magic is the art of changing consciousness at will. In this way, art and ritual work to the same purpose. Creating ceremony to honor our work, our play, our art, our lives, restores our dignity. It reminds us that it is through the everyday expression of our humanness that Great Spirit is honored, making our lives a living prayer. It heals the separation of body, mind and spirit. This altar symbolized healing that separation and the separation of women—black, white, yellow and red—from each other.

O Mitakuye Oyasin—To All My Relations
Mary Faulkner

Mary Faulkner

The Altar

Honoring the Native American people,
still homeless in their own land . . .

Mary Faulkner

Fumiliyo

She was Aunt Jemima all over, this doll. From head to toe she was both a caricature and a stereotype of a Southern house slave, stuffed and sewn and painted and dressed by a white male dollmaker in the last decade of the 20th century.

Her face was distorted, with one eye lower than the other and a large, long mouth made more grotesque and exaggerated by "many thousands" of individual teeth. Her clothing, which was sewn securely to her body, was typical for a house slave: a kerchief tied around her head, a skirt and blouse covered by a surprisingly well-made apron, and underneath, pantaloons of a much finer quality than the coarse fabric of her outer apparel. One hand held a milk pail. The other hand, fingers spread, covered her mouth.

This is how Pat Smith found her, in an upstairs shop on Nashville's Second Avenue, on a spring day in 1992. Pat, an artist, designer and teacher, was shopping with a close friend, a woman to whom she had confided her recently realized desire for a doll. As they browsed they became separated for a time, then her friend returned and spoke softly to Pat, "Your doll's upstairs, baby."

The moment Pat saw the doll she experienced a "thump, a leap, a powerful feeling" in her heart. Yes, she felt "distaste" for the doll's slave image, but at the same time she heard the doll's spirit calling to her: "Free me. Free me." And that, on many levels, is exactly what she did.

The doll's transformation from anonymous slave to African-American woman of power has become a potent personal symbol for Pat, a "vehicle through which I can implement my own transformation. She was always 'her,' much greater than an inanimate object, never just a doll." The actual act of reclaiming this doll became a deeply meaningful cooperative effort for Pat and her two daughters. "It felt like we were birthing something together."

Her name, Fumiliyo, is African. In Nigeria's Yoruba language, Fumiliyo means "give me good things." Her clothing and headdress are of fine, richly colorful African fabric. Her facial features are balanced and beautiful. The hand that once held a milk pail now holds a double terminated quartz crystal. Fumiliyo's other hand once again covers her mouth, but this time it is there to remind Pat of her need to be grounded, and to listen to her inner Self.

For a time Fumiliyo and the process of her transformation commanded Pat's attention so completely that Pat became concerned, almost afraid. Then, on a trip to New Orleans, accompanied by Fumiliyo, Pat felt compelled to write. She wrote, then wrote some more, surrendering, allowing whatever came to her to flow out through her pen and onto the paper. She found clarity and comfort when this message at last came through: "Thank you for freeing me. Don't be afraid. When I speak to you, you are not possessed by me. I am here to help you."

Fumiliyo spoke to her at length that day, addressing Pat's inner conflicts and insecurities about what directions to take in her art and in her life. Fumiliyo's counsel continues to be a source of insight, empowerment and spiritual strength for Pat, helping her to free herself from the oppression of the past, inspiring her to discover and express her own truth in her own way.

Pat was confused and discouraged when this doll came into her life, but as she has liberated the doll and restored her true identity, Pat has experienced deep inner growth and transformation. She feels more positive, more capable, more empowered. Outwardly, much has changed, too. Fumiliyo's presence in her life has truly "given her good things" which Pat had long wanted but thought impossible, beyond her reach. Now the door is opening for opportunity and abundance to flow into her life with ease, including a new car and a studio of her own.

Although Fumiliyo is very personal to her, Pat occasionally shares her doll. At Women on the Inner Journey workshops and art exhibits, Fumiliyo takes her place on the sacred altar as a powerful symbol of possibility for individual transformation and healing of the deep wounds inflicted on black women by slavery, and on all women by the continuing oppression inherent in our patriarchal society. At such times Fumiliyo's remarkable spirit is a source of light for us all.

Penny Case and Pat Smith

Art is not just an object. It is a process, and the process is a spiritual, transformative map filled with great psychic content. The ego pushes towards a receptive balance in order to keep the work moment to moment and constantly alive.

We Are All
terra cotta/found fossil
50" x 60"

Sydney Reichman

Voices in Harmony

Build a Bridge

We are sisters on a journey
Children of Mother Earth
Born to share her treasures
A sacred right by birth
But history's come between us
Dividing one and all
It's time to work together
And instead of building walls
    Build a bridge . . . heart to heart
    Let's close the distance that keeps us apart
    Build a bridge . . . black and white
    Out of the darkness and into the light
    Build a bridge . . . let's build a bridge
When we put the past behind us
We'll come to understand
There is healing in forgiveness
And the power is in our hands (to)
    Build a bridge . . . heart to heart
    Let's close the distance that keeps us apart
    Build a bridge . . . black and white
    Out of the darkness and into the light
    Build a bridge . . . let's build a bridge
    Build a bridge
    (Sisters on a journey)
    Build a bridge
    (It's time to work together)
    Build a bridge
    (Put the past behind us)
    Build a bridge
    (Sisters on a journey)
Jeannie Smith & Mary Beth Anderson
© 1992 Sweet Street Music/Miss Kitty Music

Why the Struggle

Unless my eyes are deceiving me, tell me what on earth is this I see
White man laying out in the sun trying to get a tan like me
Black man presses and straightens his hair
To look like the white man over there
If we so admire what the other has
Why can't we live
Sister, sister
Brother, brother
Why the struggle
(Why the struggle y'all?)
    Oooh we criticize, yet we imitate the other
    Why not celebrate this big rainbow of color
    Shiny black satin, soft silky white
    Ruby red sunset, and yellow moonlight
    So tell me why (tell me why)
    Why the struggle
    (Somebody tell me why the struggle)
Unless my heart is misleading me, we stir up trouble needlessly
Makes me laugh each time I see how we do the same things differently
White man wants that boom box thrill
Black man, the mansion on the hill
If we can share in each other's dreams
Why can't we live
Sister, sister
Brother, brother
Why the struggle
Why the struggle
    REPEAT CHORUS
Tell me why (tell me why)
Why the struggle
Somebody tell me (somebody tell me)
Tell me why the struggle
Why do we make trouble (somebody tell me)
Why do we criticize each other
When we could live in peace (when we could live in peace)

Vanessa Hill/Jeannie Smith/Mary Beth Anderson
© 1992 Sweet Street Music

Blossoming
computer
16" x 20"

In this piece two diverse images—the external versus the internal—are integrated through a relationship of color sensitivity, translucent layers and design. Through moving that which is spiritual toward that which is worldly, a path emerges where arms unfold and take in new insights. Growth emerges where bridges are being built and walls are breaking down, connecting differences, recognizing the interconnectedness of all things in the whole: sexuality, spirituality, black, white, male, female.

Julie Luckett

Death into Eternal Life
oil on canvas
30" x 48"

My whole objective in my art is to provoke thought and discussion about our soul's journey through the darkness. My paintings talk about different phases in my own journey, my "footprints." As you track them, you will see that though I feel lost sometimes, they are all headed toward the light.

Elizabeth Townsel

In Passing

This is not the life to cling to,
this is not the place to stay.
This is not the end of our beginning,
not the station, but the way.

This is but a passing moment
in an endless stream of time.
It's a bubble in a bathtub;
it's a circle, not a line.

We are works of art created by
painters of the soul.
We are light and shadow, moving pictures;
frames on a single roll.

The film is eternity,
the camera is life.
And we are images of God
in flickering black and white.

Gwynelle Dismukes

Building

Bridges

in Your

Community

Women Who Came Before Us

This past summer I had the opportunity to speak with two exceptional women in the Nashville community, women who have contributed to, and often created, the intentional bridge-building between black and white people going on in two spirit-centered organizations. Ms. Laura McCray, an 85-year-old social activist, spoke to me about the inherently unifying activities at Edgehill United Methodist Church, while Ms. Maxine Clark Beach told me about the empowering philosophy and programs at the Scarritt-Bennett Center, where she serves as executive director.

At the foundation of both groups is the focused intention to include, support and empower people, particularly women and people of color. Edgehill Church was founded in 1966 as the first interracial church in Nashville. The Scarritt-Bennett Center is now celebrating its 100-year heritage of empowering and educating women. It was also one of the first interracial colleges in the South. From these foundations of commitment and intention, much ground-breaking work continues and many bridges are still being built—sometimes in subtle ways, other times in more obvious ways.

As Ms. McCray spoke to me in her East Nashville home, she showed a keen awareness of the quiet undercurrents of trust and community that develop when people of different races come together to work and worship.

I loved the story of her coming to Edgehill. Laura, who was raised a Baptist, came while visiting her daughter, who had married a Methodist minister. She was taking her grandchildren for the inclusive church school experience, and was so impressed with all the ministries of the church that she joined, then and there. Laura says she told them, "I'm not going to be here but one month, but because you all are doing so many good things, I want to be part of this for one month." Her spontaneity inspired a long-time participant, Roxie Jennings, to join the church on that same day. Now, 15 years later, the two are close friends who still laugh about the shared experience.

Five years later, after joining Edgehill, Laura began a successful feeding program for the homeless called Luke 14:12 [a passage which directs us to feed those who cannot repay us.] Besides the obvious benefits, it has helped build a variety of bridges between black and white people. Twice a week, volunteers from a particular United Methodist, Baptist, Jewish or Presbyterian house of worship come together at Edgehill to prepare a meal. The helpers get to know one another by preparing and serving food for approximately 80 people. The homeless persons, always a mixed group of all ages, find a place where they can come together with respect to share a full-course meal in dignity. The relationship between the volunteers and the homeless is important, too. Some call Laura Mama, and some hug her to say thank you. "It has nothing to do with being black or white."

Laura also spoke of the potluck meetings where church members learn to appreciate one another's food, sometimes

Ms. Laura McCray

sharing an African or other cultural meal. After church on Sundays, many members gather in small groups to eat out. Not only does this nurture those who might otherwise be eating alone, it ministers to the people around them who see that "black and white people can eat together, worship together and love each other."

Edgehill also provides a place where black and white people can work together. Much of the work of the United Methodist Church is done through committees and commissions, and Laura is a member of the local group studying religion and race. They are currently studying Native Americans, and the co-chairs for this particular committee are black and white. At times, Laura may be the only African American in the group, and not notice this because "I have equal opportunity for whatever goes on here." Edgehill members also address divisions between black and white people through local workshops and retreats where they discuss issues and role-play conflicts. "We talk about how it can be solved, and then we go about solving it!"

Laura attributes part of Edgehill's success to its leadership and feels the group is blessed by its roots in inclusiveness. Founding member the Rev. Bill Barnes, who is white, serves as pastor, and the late Rev. Moses Dillard, Jr., who was black, served as associate pastor.

Like Rev. Barnes, Ms. Maxine Clark Beach was part of a local group in the early 60s who dreamed of there being an integrated church. At the time she was working on an undergraduate degree in inner city ministries at Scarritt College. She next pursued graduate study at Harvard and Boston Universities, and eventually came back to Scarritt in 1989 to accept the challenge of "taking empty buildings and turning them into a program."

After the closing of the college in the spring of 1988, the Women's Division of the United Methodist Church renovated the buildings to create a full-service lay conference center. It is now a place for nontraditional continuing education—for meetings, retreats and seminars. In keeping with the tradition of Scarritt, the Center is committed to empowering women, eradicating racism, educating the laity and promoting spiritual formation (the formation of the spiritual self through prayer, worship, meditation). It is designed as a neutral ground for non-profit groups of all kinds to gather, as well as space for the Center's own programs.

As we spoke in her office, Maxine told me the daring story of the college's integration in 1952. "They just admitted two African American women, took them through a full year of college, and announced at the end that they were given master's degrees in Christian Education. When the phone calls started and people said 'You can't do this', they simply replied, 'But we've already done it'." With this and other courageous stories in mind, Maxine told me that they strive to not only do what is right, but to model what they think is right. This exemplary and active bridge-building is apparent in both the internal and external activities of the Center.

Maxine, as founding director, builds bridges internally by doing everything in her power to hire as diverse a staff as possible from the Nashville area. Her pride was obvious when she told me stories of the talented variety of people on her staff. "It's been very interesting to see how people who have great gifts, and great skills and great capabilities have been held back, have not been allowed to be all that they are, simply because of their color."

Approximately half the people in every department are people of color in some way, "And basically, that's because we've been very intentional about it."

The Center's successful internal and external integration has brought to light the need to face our differences. Even though there are many things all people share in common, Maxine acknowledged that in getting to know people from all over the world, she finds that we are all very different. She talked about how easy it is to become afraid of that which divides us and makes us feel different, instead of accepting and celebrating the richness in our differences. Through the many programs and events the Center sponsors, the gifts of such a struggle are clear. This is a place where rich diversity is being shared and celebrated.

An excellent example is the series of weekend workshops called "Women in the Global Context." Twice a year, the Center invites 20 to 25 women from all over the world—Ethiopia, Africa, Asia, rural Appalachia, etc.—to discuss and explore a particular issue in the context of their own lives. Through sharing food, crafts, dance, drums and ritual, these very different women build bridges on many levels.

Ms. Maxine Clark Beach

Another example is the Center's huge celebration of Martin Luther King Jr.'s birthday, with music, dance and drums. Workshops are held utilizing creative and diverse people in the community, such as Karen Roberts, a teacher and choreographer of African dance.

Maxine sees this as not only a celebration of King's life, but as a way of joining together that is "more effective than words." This affirmation of the power of non-verbal expressions is also apparent in the many other progressive events the Center sponsors.

Maxine hopes to develop a multicultural arts program that helps us to be enriched by each other's culture. Another dream, one she shared with Edgehill's Rev. Dillard, is that of a Saturday school for children which cuts across class, color, cultural and religious lines. There, kids could explore music and art, and learn to love one another.

Participants in the last series of "Women in the Global Context" seminar discussed the possibility of organizing an international women's fair. Maxine wants to bring together Kurdish, Asian and other women in the community who are struggling to preserve their culture, and would like to share out of their heritage. The fair would help build community among diverse women, and hopefully serve as a medium for sharing personal stories. Maxine believes this sharing can be a healing act—acknowledging the value of each woman's unique journey and personal history.

Like all women, Maxine and Laura, too, have different and valuable stories to tell. They have traveled different journeys, but in many ways have come to a common road to forge the same bridge.

Their approaches are a bit different, as are their guiding words. Laura told me early in our conversation that the words *faith* and *grace* have helped her "come this far." Maxine shared her closing words with gravity. "We live in an unjust world unless we practice justice, and we have to work very hard at that."

Both women and the organizations they represent have shown a motivating desire for true integration and true sharing. The bridges they continue to build may be as simple as sharing a meal or as dynamic as dancing out our differences. All are important and all hold their own blessings. May the rich sharing and exploring of diversity continue in mutual respect, and with deep celebration.

Ellen LaPenna

My most recent series of paintings deal with semiology. These oil and acrylic paintings on wood examine the theory of signs and symbols. These artworks explore symbols and their functions both in an artificially constructed paradigm as well as in a natural environment.

Three Conversations About Love
acrylic on wood
42 x 15 x 3

Victoria Boone

Bridging Hearts—Guidelines

Since this project began last year there has been a nationwide increase in activity regarding racial issues. Many individuals and institutions have expressed interest in participating in this project. We are being invited to bring the art show and performance to schools, galleries and businesses, and often I am asked to create workshops for other communities wanting to begin the process I have started here.

There is an increased desire on the part of other cities, groups and institutions to build bridges not only between black and white, but with other races, too. There is little information about this work, and few models exist. I offer these guidelines based on my own experience creating this project, including sharing some of my difficulties and mistakes.

COMMITMENT

It is very important that you be aware of the amount of time, energy and economic support necessary to bring people together in this way. When you are working on an all-volunteer basis, people will come and go in their free time. You, however, may have to put energy into the project most of the time. Where financial support is available, perhaps you can be paid for some of your time, but be prepared to give a lot without material compensation.

GUIDANCE

Whether you are an individual or an institution, how you will create your bridge depends on your particular interest or field of work. This process is not limited to artists. It can be done in every field of human life.

I designed this project around my personal resources for executing it: I am an artist, and I work in healing, also. When you create your own project, it is vitally important to carefully select an expert, someone who is already working in the field of healing and interracial issues. Keep in mind that, whether you are white, black or mulatto, this is a very painful issue. Bringing the races together must be done carefully, by people who know what they are doing.

Great care should be taken from the beginning. This is a process that can be done only with people who are ready and willing to dedicate time and energy to a process that does not bring economic reward.

Each group should receive information about the project from someone they trust, probably someone of their own race. Keep in mind that this whole idea of bridging the races is potentially insulting to both black and white.

SUPPORT

Identify people in your community who are already building bridges among races. These can be your key people. They understand what this process is about and usually provide the group with a great example of free interactions with other races. Identify, too, local institutions and organizations involved in interracial work. They can be very helpful in supporting your project and may also benefit each other.

I encourage you to create a core group of people who truly believe that healing racial wounds is absolutely essential for the survival of humanity and, particularly, for this country. I found that people who had an authentic spiritual practice in their lives were the ones who stood beside me all the time.

COMMITTEES

In the first meeting with the people involved, be very clear about the emotional implications of this type of project, and the time commitment it requires. Make your people aware that projects of this nature do not progress in a predictable, orderly way. The process of unfolding is one of unexpected twists and surprising new directions. It is often difficult for people to adjust to such spontaneity. Help them to be prepared.

What the responsibilities of each member will be depends on the kind of project you are creating. This project had many needs: fundraising, publicity, mailing, food and drink, typesetting, graphic design and more. If your needs are similar, plan to create committees and work with many people. If your project is limited to meetings and workshops, the needs and implications will be more simple.

Many things have changed since I started this project. Last year the idea of building bridges between black and white was an almost untouchable issue. Many people were in denial until the riot occurred in Los Angeles and subsequent information revealed what is really going on.

Many people now realize that segregation is not yet over. I heard white people say, "Oh! I didn't think the situation was still so terrible in black communities. I supposed that was over." Many white people have been able to believe the problems between the races are over because they live in protected places where the only blacks are those who come to clean the house nicely and quietly.

Finally, the new administration in Washington is creating an new example of respect, validation and acknowledgement not only for blacks, but for other races, too. I have a sense that both black and white people are perceiving this government model as permission to make efforts like this project. People are beginning to understand that only if we make these efforts will change happen.

Noris Binet

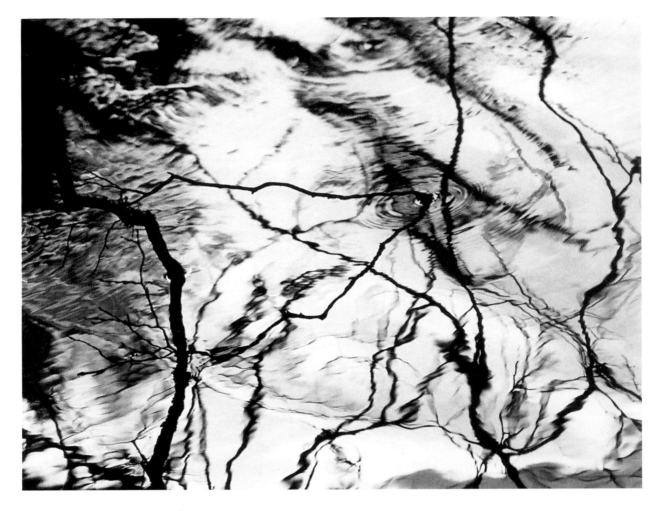

The Goddess Speaks
photography
10" x 13"

From childhood I have been fascinated by running water. Water is life-giving. Our earliest creation myths tell us of a goddess coming out of the sea and bringing life into the world. When I saw the water tumbling over the rocks, I knew I had to see the Goddess. My photographs of the Goddess are steps on my own Inner Journey.

Elizabeth Papousek

contra/indications in terms

here we are
living our art
some of us dreamers
some nightmare-walkers
some of us artists
living our art
as we become
our own living art
we take ourselves back
to the start
to the heart
of thou art

(art: human effort to imitate,
supplement, alter, or counter-
act the work of nature)

The differences can only be dissolved
when each can look through the other's eyes,
and both can surrender
to the one self they find.

Gwynelle Dismukes

Appendix

Artists

MARY BETH ANDERSON European-American artist. Born in New York State. Raised in the Catskill Mountains, where her father directed a summer camp for urban children, giving her "a good balance of ethnic awareness" at an early age. This awareness grew during her teen years when she lived with her family at Columbia University on the edge of New York City's racially mixed Harlem. "Since coming to Nashville and being part of the country music scene my circle of relationships has been 99 percent white." After learning of this project during one of Noris Binet's therapeutic dance classes, she and Jeannie Smith offered to write a song for the first opening. More music has followed. "This has been a life changing project for me. I will never forget the thrill of seeing those at the opening, hand in hand, singing each word to 'Build A Bridge.' It was concept in action. Who knows where this journey will take us . . . I hope to help us get there."

LYNDA BATES European-American participant. A native Texan, she has resided in Tennessee for four years. She was surprised and disappointed, upon arrival in Tennessee, to see and experience people's prejudice; especially relating to black people. She was directed toward this project by an African-American woman friend and joined the effort to help reduce this prejudice through public education, using art as the medium.

NORIS BINET Afro-Caribbean artist. Born and raised in the Dominican Republic. She studied art and architecture there, then moved to Mexico in 1976, at age 20, to continue her education. "This culture fascinated me so deeply that I can really say that it is my spiritual home. It was through my involvement with the Native American cultures I learned about the integration of mind, body and spirit. While formally studying sociology, I continued my personal investigation of contemporary psychological theories, especially those derived from Wilhelm Reich and Carl Jung, and I continued my own work with dreams, folklore, expressive arts, ritual and ceremony. In 1989 I moved to Nashville, a new phase of my personal voyage. My work here is focused on the interrelationship of art, healing and spirituality."

VICTORIA BOONE European-American artist. She holds a Master of Liberal Studies degree with Museum Emphasis from the University of Oklahoma, and a B.F.A. from the University of Alabama in Tuscaloosa. She is Director of Visual Arts, Crafts and Media with the Tennessee Arts Commission, and an active participant in and consultant for many national art programs. Her photography and painting have been widely exhibited and published. "I believe this project increased the level of consciousness in Nashville. Through art, linkages have been made among women of different races which will raise networking possibilities."

JANE BRADDOCK European-American artist. "I was born in Indiana, raised in Connecticut, got a B.F.A. from Syracuse University in 1968. After 15 years in New York City, I moved to Tennessee, where I now paint in a tin studio with coral columns in the woods. Always interested in exhibitions, I was especially intrigued with the premise and process of this show. Painting is a solitary act. I saw this as an opportunity to connect artistically, emotionally and spiritually with first a select group of women, then with the greater community. These are missing links in the Western art paradigm. Inclusion and communication, the humanizing of art is perhaps a distinctly female offering, and one to which I want to contribute."

BARBARA BULLOCK African-American artist. "Born in 1946, before the Civil Rights movement, I have seen, firsthand, the devastating effects of the blatant prejudice of mental and physical intimidation take their toll on the otherwise bright and gifted members of my family and community. I have seen the same thing happen to women. Although I have majored in fine arts at Nashville's Peabody College, it has taken me decades to realize my self-worth. This project has challenged me to face the very painful reasons that keep women of the separate races from bonding together to overcome our shared problems. It has brought the artists a step closer in understanding and tolerance, and given us the strength to create an ideal America where every person can be encouraged and appreciated for her own individual merits."

PENNY CASE European-American artist. Born in Colorado, lived in the West 40 years before moving to Tennessee in 1982. A graduate of the University of Denver, she is a writer and a holistic animal health practitioner. Through her work with Noris Binet, she has discovered she is also an artist. "This project is creating healing at the very roots of our society. Healing on such a deep level gives us new options for a better future."

MINISA CRUMBO Native American artist. Born September, 1942, Tulsa, Oklahoma, of Pottawatomi and Creek American Indian descent. She is the daughter of internationally known Indian artist Woody Crumbo and Lillian Hogue Crumbo, an educator. Her work has been exhibited worldwide, and is in a number of permanent collections, including the Heard Museum, Phoenix, Arizona, and the Pushkin Museum, Moscow.

GWYNELLE DISMUKES African-American artist. She is a poet, a free-lance writer and a mother of two. With regard to the Black and White project she says, "This process of healing the wounds between people is not all one of loving, sharing and good feelings. There is a lot of anger and deep resentments which must be squarely faced, as well as the continuing realities of the world to which we must return from the spiritual realm of our workshops. I feel that with my work I provide a reminder of those realities, and a balance between the progress we experience here and the great work remaining to be done within our society."

JOHNNIE ENLOE European-American artist. Born in Louisiana, she lived there and in Arkansas until moving to Nashville recently. "I learned about life through my family"—an education she now pursues with four grandchildren—as well as through 15 years in the workplace and volunteer drug and alcohol prevention work with adolescents. "The visual arts came as an outlet for severe stress 20 years ago and I found that art is life and life through art is my great inner teacher. Joining with other women on the inner journey has fulfilled a long sought-after dream of breaking down racial and cultural walls."

MARY FAULKNER European-American artist. She holds a master's degree in religious education from Scarritt College with a special focus in Liberation Theology and women's spirituality. She has practiced Earth Religion for many years. Her mentors include: Buck Ghosthorse, Lakota Sioux Medicine Man; Luisha Teish, Priestess of Oshun in the Yoruba Tradition of Africa; Starhawk, M.A., Pagan Priestess; and Carol Christ, Ph.D., Theology, Yale University. She attended the International Institute for Women's Studies in Greece and Turkey, where she studied the Goddess Period and the art of ritual. She currently lives in Nashville, where she writes, and has a counseling practice using a process of inner journeys to uncover creativity and locate personal wisdom.

JANE FLEISHMAN European-American artist. "I was born and raised in Arizona. From there, 'the South' seemed as remote as a foreign country to me. However, when I finished college in Ohio, I followed a friend to Nashville, Tennessee, and have lived there almost continuously since 1977. I am married and have one son. Most of my professional life I have spent working on issues related to poverty and injustice. A few years ago I began to work on my own issues—my own inner poverty, you might say. Art played, and still plays, an important part in my inner work. I am very grateful I was able to become involved with this project because it allowed me to begin to bring together my newly emerged artist-self and my activist-self."

JOAN FRENCH European-American film producer. A Nashville native. Her work includes documentaries, music videos, commercials and promotional films. Her concern with healing race relations began with the Civil Rights Movement in 1963. She was a founding member of DARE (Direct Action for Racial Equality) in Raleigh, North Carolina. Through her involvement in the movement, she became interested in religious mysticism, and for more than 20 years has studied with teachers of Zen and Tibetan Buddhism, Western Tantric Yoga and the Esoteric Cherokee tradition. Currently, she is developing a documentary project on spiritual music throughout the world.

VANESSA HILL African-American artist. Born in Detroit, Michigan, the 11th of 12 children, but raised in the rural South, she grew up ' with a dream and desire to spread love and peace through music and song." The music industry drew her to Nashville, where she is working to manifest that dream. "I feel that music is the one sure way to reach people. I don't know anyone young or old, black, white, red or yellow who doesn't enjoy some form of music. I am proud to be a part of Women on the Inner Journey, organized by Noris Binet, another dreamer in action."

MARYANNE HOWLAND was born "an underprivileged youth" in Cleveland, Ohio's inner city. Recently relocated to the Nashville area from Manhattan, MaryAnne is the president of her own marketing firm, which has offices in New York and Nashville. "I remember seeing tanks rolling down St. Clair Avenue from 105th Street during the riots in 1968. After the 10:00 neighborhood curfew, anyone found walking in the streets was stopped, questioned and harassed or "dissed" by armed guardsmen. I'll never forget the sight of flames shooting up over houses. That was the view from our back porch. Shortly after that, James Brown came out with 'Say It Loud, I'm Black and I'm Proud.' I've been saying it ever since. I got involved with this project first because Noris is my friend and she asked me to. Without ever having attended her workshop or an opening, but by the very nature of the writings and the art in this book, I was inspired and compelled to write 'The Color of Blood.' It is still, and will always be, a work in progress."

ELLEN LAPENNA European-American writer. A Nashville native, she has worked as a freelance promotional writer since graduating from Memphis State University. Her interest in this project stems from her "desire to learn about, and to affirm the dignity of African-Americans so there may be mutual sharing."

RENEE LAROSE European-American artist. An honors graduate of the Otis/Parsons School of Art and Design in Los Angeles, she is now a full-time studio artist, and is currently on the faculty of Watkins Institute of the Nashville School of Art. Her award-winning, socially conscious work is widely exhibited. "This project was a dream come true for me. All over the world, growing up without prejudice is almost impossible. As children, we are victims, easily influenced by the prejudice of those we most look up to. For those of us who have awakened to this atrocity, it is an exciting opportunity to walk down a different path, or carve that path in hopes that one day it will turn into an international freeway."

DORI LEMEH African-American artist. A Nashville native. After graduating from Tennessee State University, she went on to earn a Master of Fine Arts degree from Pennsylvania State University, where she is now Assistant Professor of Art. Her widely exhibited art explores the multilayered, spiritual relationship between people and nature. She loves teaching art, an experience she says helped her discover what she really wants to create. "When I began teaching, my personal philosophy of painting began to take shape. Now I can go to the canvas with more intent and direction. It enhances my work. As much as I give to the students, they reciprocate."

NINA LOVELACE African-American artist. Born in Florence, Alabama. Educated at Fisk University, Illinois State University and the Skowhegan School of Painting and Sculpture. Currently on the faculty of the Department of Art, Tennessee State University. "I came to this project because I was excited about the idea of women making a conscious choice to unite and use our powers to heal. The opportunity to do this through art is important not only because images can reveal our afflictions, but also because visions of wholeness can help to bring into existence the perfect souls which we really are. This is the power of art so often missed in many academic approaches, yet this power is at art's very core. The workshop was an avenue for me to affirm what I believe is an essential function of art."

JULIE LUCKETT European-American artist. A native Nashvillian. "Blossoming into a woman, I saw my artwork take shape in self-exploration." She was drawn to Women on the Inner Journey "through serendipity and synchronicity." "Growing up in the South, I developed prejudices which I care not to have. I have questioned my place as a woman living in the South from all angles. But rather than seeing myself as a victim of society, I take full responsibility for myself and choose to perfect and evolve what my society has given me, owning my own power."

MARGARET L. MEGGS European-American feminist theologian and ritualist. Since 1986 she has been director of Womanflight, an organization offering women opportunities to explore the intersection of feminism and spirituality. She has developed and taught courses in women's spirituality, ritual, meditation, sacred circle dance, women in ministry and women's religious history. She is also on the staff of the Women's Studies Program at Vanderbilt University, and teaches Women's Studies at Middle Tennessee State University. Margaret created the altar for the Women on the Inner Journey exhibit. She cared for the altar during the Black and White opening, and created altars for for the Harpeth Hall (Nashville) and Bowling Green, Kentucky, openings of that exhibit.

ELIZABETH PAPOUSEK European-American artist. She recalls that, as a child growing up in Charlotte, North Carolina, she "knew that racial segregation was wrong and oppressive." After receiving her B.A. from Duke University, she left the South, intending to return only to visit family. She earned an M.S. from the University of Iowa, a Ph.D from UCLA, and was teaching at the University of Montana when she was invited to teach at historically black Fisk University in Nashville. I accepted, expecting to stay only a year or so. I have been at Fisk for over 20 years." Artistic expression became part of her life when, following her daughter's college graduation, she began studying photography. Her work is widely exhibited. "I joined Women on the Inner Journey because I saw the possibility of verbal and visual creative sharing in a biracial group."

SYDNEY REICHMAN European-American artist. "Born 1950, Nashville, Tennessee. Colleges, travel to Europe and Israel looking for home. Found clay and sculpture. Built a hand-made house from the ground up. Reclaimed the abused land that surrounded it. Discovered color in my gardens which evolved into painting where I am now. Why this project? Southern Jew in the 50's growing up in a blue-eyed blond ostracizing world. The richest, most safe place was with my Dad and his best friend, James Miller. James was black. You might say that colored my vision from the beginning."

ANGELA J. SMITH European-American artist. Writer and designer, born and raised in the middle Tennessee area. Graduating from Belmont College with a B.A. in Communications, she has worked in the communications industry as a Graphic Designer and Electronic Communications Specialist. "Building Bridges is the central focus of my life, my life calling. The key to building the bridges is communicating from the heart, communicating visually and verbally. I am a woman on an inner journey, and the inner journey is manifesting itself externally in this project." She is a key person in the conception and production of this product.

JEANNIE SMITH European-American artist. "Creating songs for this project has opened up an inner pathway which has allowed many thoughts and feelings about who I am as a woman to pass through. I believe these same thoughts and feelings dwell in the heart of every woman. It is my hope that these songs will touch their hearts, bringing to the surface all the things we share as women, for it is much easier to Build a Bridge on common ground."

PAT SMITH African-American artist. Nashville native. An early interest in art remained dormant until, at 38, she returned to school, earning a degree in Studio Art from Tennessee State University. Rediscovering her creativity "resulted in a tremendous physical, spiritual and emotional healing and awakening," and a desire to "assist others on their journey of self-discovery." With her Master of Education degree from Peabody College of Vanderbilt University, she has been teaching art in Nashville's Antioch High School. Pat believes "the healing that must take place on this planet can be initiated through women and children. I welcome the opportunity to open myself on a soul level to those women willing to do likewise in order to affect healing of one of the most vicious diseases of our society . . . racism. Part of my task is, through my art, to raise awareness of the many ignored contributions other cultures have made to our civilization."

HEATHER THOMPSON European-American artist. Born 1955, Ridgetop, Tennessee. Lives in Nashville with her two children. "Life as I know it began a few months before Sacred Circle Dance started in November 1985. I have since gradually awakened myself to the work I want to do, which is living fully, with intent to touch every mind and body I can in order to help awaken that spirit within. This project helped me connect with other women—earth-centered Spiritual Women. Together we share a higher purpose of healing and transforming ourselves and society. Together we are helping to create a balance of color about which I have felt so strongly since childhood."

MARY ELIZABETH TOWNSEL African-American artist. An expressionist painter, born and raised in Chicago, Illinois, now living in Brentwood, Tennessee. After three children and a divorce, she returned to school, attending I.I.T., American Academy of Art, and Chicago Columbia College. She became very ill in 1982, a result of severe stress. Turning inward, she began a process of self-healing and spiritual transformation. Eight years later she attended a gallery opening of "Images from the Unconscious." The artist? Noris Binet. There it was, a strong body of work dealing with spiritual vision. At that moment she knew the direction her art would take. "I believe the entire process of changing the world, and especially building bridges for humanity, must begin with the self. By gaining knowledge and acceptance of the self, we begin the process of learning to love and affirm ourselves and each other."

VIOLA WOOD African-American artist. Born in Nashville. A ceramic sculptor and educator, she is a graduate of Fisk University, holds Master of Arts and Master of Fine Arts degrees from Northern Illinois University, and completed additional studies at Arizona State University and Arromont School of Arts and Crafts. Her widely exhibited sculpture is inspired by objects used in traditional African religious and cultural ceremonies. She joined Women on the Inner Journey "to meet, exchange ideas and exhibit with a group of women artists from diverse ethnic backgrounds. The sharing of spiritual and intellectual ideas was a wonderfully intriguing experience."

The Author

photograph by Carlton Wilkinson

Noris Binet is an artist, sociologist, and facilitator in therapeutic dance. She was born in the Caribbean island of the Dominican Republic in 1956. She moved to Nashville in 1989 after living in Mexico for thirteen years.

Binet is the creator of the *Women on the Inner Journey* organization, and the *Black and White Building a Bridge* multimedia project. Her concern is not only with healing racial wounds between black and white, but in creating bridges of communication between the first world and the third world.

She believes that now is the moment when both cultures need to meet in a safe and sacred place where true communication can happen. Women from both cultures have something to teach and something to learn from each other. She calls this process "human ecology." "We can't save the planet if we don't save our cultures, and the humanity in each one of us. We are not separate from nature, we are part of it."

In this book she expresses her cross-cultural perspective, giving us another view about how we can explore a more respectful attitude to other races and develop a perception of the world as a whole. She feels all cultures need to truly open their hearts to create together, because the destiny of this world is a responsibility of all.

Women On The Inner Journey offers a variety of ongoing workshops facilitated by Noris Binet for those wishing to explore spirituality and healing. Participants experience unblocking of the creative energy through dance, movement, expressive arts and ritual. This multi-media project *Black and White Women Building a Bridge* includes the following, and is available to your community: Art Exhibit, Performance, Workshop, and Video Presentation.

WORKSHOPS by Noris Binet

Black and White Building a Bridge

African Americans and European Americans exploring racial healing.
It is not enough to talk about it, but to experience it, to live it.
(groups for women only, and for men and women)

Women on the Inner Journey: Therapeutic Dance

Women searching for their spiritual identities. Exploring the multifaceted healing potentials in the rhythmic movement of the body.

"Awakening the Healer": For Women Who Are Not Mothers

An exploration of the spiritual role of these women, and the creation of a space for them both in their own lives and in today's society. The shamanic path.

Human Ecology

Beginning Winter, 1993, a week-long journey of transformation and discovery in tropical Mar de Jade, Mexico, on the Pacific Coast. A women's multicultural workshop for cross-cultural awareness, personal transformation and restoring respect for our planet and its inhabitants through a spiritual understanding of the shamanic ways of our ancestors. Available November, December, January and February. Limited to 20 women.

Women on the Inner Journey is a non-profit organization seeking funding.
For information on workshops, or to order videos or additional copies of this book, contact:

Women on the Inner Journey
P.O. Box 41761
Nashville, Tennessee 37204
(615) 297-6654

Sponsors

We are thankful to the following sponsors of this book for enabling us to have a voice, and for believing in our efforts to humanize our culture.

VERY SPECIAL THANKS
LifeWorks Foundation
Scarritt-Bennett Center

MAJOR SPONSORS
Keith Case and Associates
RCA Records
In The Gallery

CONTRIBUTING SPONSORS
Prime Focus
With Any Luck Music
Stephen L. Reisman, MD
Joanne Singer
Art and Soul
Besway
Body Conscious
Karen T. Callis, LCSN
Kristy Combs
Gale Carrier, Psychic Consultant
Dragonfly Books
Jackie Dixon/Mary Kay Cosmetics
Futons Unfolding
Four Seasons Travel Center, Inc.
Innerlight Metaphysics
Institute for Integrative Healing Arts
Jayem Associates
Kowalski Chiropractic
Kraft Brothers, Esstman, Patton & Harrell
Magical Journey
Amy Martin

Monette Rebecca
Mine Shaft
Diane Pate/Tri-State Rehab
The Quiet Touch
Rape and Sexual Abuse Center
Religious Science of Nashville
Frances Roy and Associates
Joel W. Solomon, Jr.
Tri-State Rehab and Case Management
A Thousand Faces
Virginia Team/Graphic Design
James S. Weinger, CPA
Where'd You Get Your Graphics
BURNT (Bring Urban Recycling to Nashville Today)
Circle Dance
College Crib
Mr. Kerry Donaldson
Mr. Steven Donaldson
Ted Jones
Diane LaPenna
Dr. Bobby Lovett
Randy Mack
Refus and Fredonia Marable
Max Mendelsohn
Stacy Miller
Dr. Willie Myers
Gregory and Gloria Ridley
Stephanie Schuttera
Sunshine Grocery
Teena Shirts

Credits

Penny Case	Editor	Joan French	Video Producer
Angela Smith	Design and Production	Sharon R. Cohen	Director
Julie Luckett	Color Correction	Dene Berry	Camera person
Laura Flippen	Associate Editor	Karen Martin	Camera person
Ellen LaPenna	Associate Editor	Suzanne Cobb	Gaffer
MaryAnne Howland	Consultant	Heather Hawthorne	Production Coordinator
Donna J. Gillroy	Fundraiser	Richard Jegen	Editor

Epilogue

We are the Bridge

Experiencing the unfolding of this project was very meaningful for me. It was a laboratory in which I explored the interaction of the forces between these two races, and how each changes when it comes into contact with the other. This has given me a deeper understanding of American culture, with its contradictions and its richness.

For many of these women, this process inspired a change in the direction of their work and in their commitment to their own healing.

I saw white women willing to turn their faces back to the European lands of their predecessors, to explore their ancestral roots. This is a very important step, because it is hard for some of them to accept that they are part of a race that has inflicted such pain on other races.

When acceptance occurs, a fundamental aspect of this process can take place: forgiveness. Forgiveness brings new, fresh perception about ourselves and about those around us, too. For some women, the challenging question became "How can I make a difference now?"

People say everything has a price. From the Native Americans, I learned we must always make an offering. I have come to realize that the price white people need to pay, the offering they are called on to make in this healing process, is not necessarily only money, but the time and the courage to connect with black people, to share their advantages and privileges so both races can explore together the development of the human consciousness.

The contribution of slaves gave the white culture much more than material wealth. Aspects of black culture seeped into the larger society, enriching it and giving it greater diversity. It is important now for the community of alternative therapists, artists and healers to build bridges with the black culture. This is an obligation, the paying back of an old debt.

Now we are in a time of sharing, and white people must come to terms with the idea that, in a capitalistic system, wealth is the result of exploitation.

My interaction with black people through this project brought me interesting insights. For those who were ready, the project provided an opportunity to explore rage and forgiveness. Finally they were able to be close to a few who belonged to this massive white dominating society and to express their feelings in a safe way in the presence of those individuals. It is difficult to forgive in the abstract; a little easier to forgive another human being. For some, their art became the perfect place to express forgotten and unspeakable emotions. It was like finding a new vein.

It was very difficult for the majority of black women to participate in this process. In this case, too, there is an offering to be made. I think what black women are called on to accept is that most of them are of mixed race. I know the pain and shame that comes with this issue. It is so important to remember, not only of pain are we made, but of passion and fire, too. Black women need to reclaim within themselves the white heritage that, genetically, they carry. When that happens, surprising change will take place. When we can embrace all the races we are made of we move to the place where we are the bridge.

We are part of the great circle of the universe—birth, death and rebirth. In that circle we are just one, without boundaries. All of us, without exception, finally come back to the earth, disintegrate in her, and nourish her with our flesh.

Black and White Women Building a Bridge is a way to start planting seeds that will, of course, take time to grow. But time is not the issue for me. I hope it is not the issue for this society, either. What must happen will find its own time. We are working for eternity.

Now is the moment to take serious steps to fill the gap, bridge the chasm between races, if American society is to survive. This can be done only by creating the spaces and conditions where true integration can occur, where all races that share the land, the air, the resources of this great continent can work together. This is just the beginning. With you, it will become whole.

Noris Binet

From the Mother of the Earth

to the new generations
for them to receive the Land
with less prejudice, less poison,
less violence . . .
The act of this group of women is
an action of grace,
hopefully with the seed of a new order,
a new understanding . . .
where it matters not what is your color,
you are still my sister/my brother.